WRITING POWER 3

Writing Fluency • Language Use • Academic Writing • Social and Professional Writing

Sue Peterson

Dorothy Zemach

Writing Power 3

Pearson Education, 10 Bank Street, White Plains, NY 10606

Staff credits: The people who made up the *Writing Power 3* team, representing editorial, production, design, and manufacturing, are Rosa Chapinal, Aerin Csigay, Dave Dickey, Nancy Flaggman, Ann France, Shelley Gazes, Amy McCormick, Liza Pleva, Massimo Rubini, and Jaimie Scanlon.

Cover images: Shutterstock.com
Text composition: TSI Graphics
Text font: 11.5/13 Adobe Caslon
Credits: See page 277

Library of Congress Cataloging-in-Publication Data
Blanchard, Karen Lourie
  Writing power. 1 : language use social and personal writing, academic writing, vocabulary building / Karen Blanchard.
    p. cm.
  ISBN 0-13-231484-3—ISBN 0-13-231485-1—ISBN 0-13-231486-X—ISBN 0-13-231487-8
  1. English language—Textbooks for foreign speakers.   2. English language—Rhetoric—Problems, exercises, etc.   3. Report writing—Problems, exercises, etc.   I. Title.
  PE1128.B5874   2012
  428.2'4—dc23

                                                                        2012006120

ISBN-10: 0-13-231486-X
ISBN-13: 978-0-13-231486-2

Printed in the United States of America
1 2 3 4 5 6 7 8 9 10—V011—17 16 15 14 13 12

Contents

Acknowledgments

The authors would like to acknowledge Beatrice S. Mikulecky and Linda Jeffries for their innovations in the *Reading Power* series, and the Pearson team for all of their efforts and contributions in making the *Writing Power* series a reality, especially Paula Van Ells, Amy McCormick, Massimo Rubini, and series co-author Karen Blanchard. A special thanks goes to Development Editor Jaimie Scanlon, whose keen mind and insights were invaluable in the shaping of this text.

Sue Peterson would also like to thank J.H. Daily for his application essay contribution. She is also deeply grateful to her family, friends, students, and colleagues including Mark, Greta, Martha, Marge, Roxa, and Patti. Finally, to her children, Sean, Jack, and Carolyn, and husband, Dan, thank you for all your patience, support, and encouragement.

Writing Power 3 **Reviewers:**
The publisher would like to extend special thanks to the following individuals who reviewed *Writing Power* and whose comments were instrumental in developing this series.

Jeff Bette, Naugatuck Valley Community College; **Leslie Biaggi,** Miami-Dade Community College; **Linda Ciano,** American Language Institute, New York University; **Sally C. Gearhart,** Santa Rosa Community College; **Anthony Halderman,** Cuesta College, San Luis Obispo, CA; **Melissa L. Parisi,** Westchester Community College; **Jason Tannenbaum,** Pace University; **Joe Walther,** Korea

About the Authors

Sue Peterson has been in the TESOL field for twenty years and is currently the assistant director of the English Language Institute of St. John's University in New York City. She has taught reading, writing, listening, speaking, and grammar to college-level students and designed numerous courses. She has been a teacher trainer in the United States and Mexico and is a regular presenter at conferences. She holds a master's degree in TESOL from Hunter College, City University of New York, and her interests are in materials development, curriculum design, and technology.

Dorothy E. Zemach has taught ESL for over 18 years, in Asia, Africa, and the United States. She holds an MA in TESL from the School for International Training in Vermont, USA. Now she concentrates on writing and editing ELT materials and textbooks and conducting teacher training workshops. Her areas of specialty and interest are teaching writing, teaching reading, business English, academic English, testing, and humor. She is a frequent plenary speaker at international conferences, and a regular blogger for Teacher Talk at http://www.azargrammar.com.

Introduction to *Writing Power 3*

To the Teacher

Writing Power 3 is unlike most other writing textbooks. Rather than focusing on one area of writing, such as fluency, language use, academic writing, or professional writing, *Writing Power 3* includes all of them to give students practical skills for writing in many different situations. The book is also organized in a different way. It contains four separate Parts that concentrate on four important aspects of writing proficiency; therefore it is like four books in one. The book's structure is flexible, allowing you to assign work from different sections of the book concurrently and to target your students' greatest needs.

The four Parts of *Writing Power 3* are:

- **Part 1: Writing Fluency**
- **Part 2: Language Use**
- **Part 3: Academic Writing**
- **Part 4: Social and Professional Writing**

Writing Power 3 is designed to meet the needs of students in pre-college programs, college bridge programs, or college or university classes. As a result, it places an emphasis on the skills necessary for academic success. *Writing Power 3* is intended for students at the intermediate to upper-intermediate level.

The purpose of *Writing Power 3* is to develop students' writing skills for a variety of purposes. Exercises target both accuracy and fluency and give students the tools they need to express themselves in effective and interesting ways. Students learn appropriate vocabulary and structures for academic, professional, and social settings, as well as techniques for creative writing.

Students also work on writing fluency throughout the course, through journal and blog assignments. The Writing Power Blog can be found at **http://pearsonELT.com/writingpowerblog**. Log on to see instructions for how to set up a private class blog, where your students can post writing assignments and communicate with classmates in a fun online environment. The Further Practice boxes throughout the book give ideas for blog assignments, as well as journal topics and research projects.

A typical unit focuses on a central topic or theme and guides students through the full writing process. Students work individually, in pairs, and in groups to:

- Brainstorm ideas
- Select, organize, and develop ideas
- Draft a text
- Check and revise the text
- "Publish" their work by sharing it with classmates and/or you

The final Writing Task at the end of the unit integrates all of the skills presented. To close the unit, students use the Check Your Writing checklist to review and revise their writing.

A separate Teacher's Guide contains the answer key, a rationale for the approach taken in *Writing Power 3*, specific suggestions for using it in the classroom, and a sample syllabus.

The authors hope you and your students will enjoy using *Writing Power 3*.

To the Student

Writing is an important part of academic, social, and professional life, both on paper and online. *Writing Power 3* teaches you skills to improve your writing in all of these areas. You will work on writing both fluently (quickly and easily) and accurately (correctly and appropriately).

This book is different from other writing textbooks. *Writing Power 3* is divided into four Parts. Instead of working on one part at a time, as in most books, you can and should work regularly on all four parts of the book.

Part 1: Writing Fluency To improve your writing fluency, it is important to write as often as you can about topics you are interested in. Units such as "Keeping a Journal" and "Blogging" will help you learn to write more quickly and easily and feel comfortable expressing yourself in writing. On the Writing Power Blog, located at **http://pearsonELT.com/writingpowerblog**, you and your classmates can post comments and have fun writing in English.

Part 2: Language Use This Part helps you work on writing more correctly. You will learn how to build your active vocabulary for writing, expand sentences, and connect ideas. These skills will help you express your ideas clearly and effectively in writing.

Part 3: Academic Writing In this Part, you will learn strategies for preparing to write, organizing ideas, and writing a full academic essay. The unit on "Revising and Proofreading" gives strategies for correcting and polishing your final work. The "Timed Essays" unit gives important skills for writing essays in timed situations such as exams.

Part 4: Social and Professional Writing This Part covers the world of work and business. Units include "Social Networking," "Business Letters," "Writing Reviews," "Current Events," and "College Application Essays."

The authors hope you will enjoy studying with *Writing Power 3*!

Begin by taking the Writing Questionnaire on the next page.

Questionnaire

What Does Writing Mean to You?

A. *Complete this questionnaire about writing in your life.*

Writing Questionnaire

Name: _____ First Language: _____

1. What kinds of things do you write in your first language? In English? Check (✓) your answers. Add other ideas.

	In your language	In English
Blog posts		
Business letters		
Chat (online)		
Emails		
Diary or journal		
Essays or compositions		
Memos		
Online reviews		
Personal letters		
Reports		
Research papers		
Text messages		
Other (add your own):		
Other (add your own):		

2. Do you enjoy writing in your first language? What is easy about it for you? What is challenging? _____

_____

3. Do you enjoy writing in English? What is easy about it for you? What is challenging?

_____

_____

4. What kinds of writing do you think you will do in English in the future? What skills might you need to do them? _____

_____

B. *Work in a group. Discuss and compare your answers to the questionnaire.*

PART

1

Writing Fluency

Introduction

ACCURACY AND FLUENCY

Writing *accurately* means using correct English and paying attention to things like grammar, vocabulary, spelling, and formatting. It can also mean following certain rules, such as indenting and beginning a paragraph with a topic sentence. Writing accurately is important when you are writing for an audience—a teacher, an employer, or any other reader for whom you need to communicate your ideas clearly.

It is also important to learn how to write *fluently*—to write quickly and easily and to express your ideas freely. Fluent writing usually expresses more of your unique "voice."

Fluency is a good skill to practice when you write for yourself, for example, in a journal. Practicing fluent writing can help you learn to complete writing tasks more quickly and feel less stress when you write, even when you are writing accurately, such as for an exam or an assignment for school.

To be a good writer, you need both accuracy and fluency. Many of the exercises in this book focus on accuracy. For those exercises, you will need your teacher's help to answer questions and check your work. However, you will also practice writing fluently by doing regular fluency writing tasks both in class and outside of class on your own.

This Part of *Writing Power 3* introduces three ways to work on your writing fluency:

- Keeping a journal
- Blogging (See page vi for information about the Writing Power Blog)
- Creative writing

A. *Read these sentences. Do they relate to accurate writing or fluent writing? Write* **A** *(accurate) or* **F** *(fluent). Write* **AF** *if you think it relates to both.*

_____ **1.** You check the spelling of words in a dictionary.

_____ **2.** You write several drafts.

_____ **3.** You write a quick email to a friend.

_____ **4.** You don't know a word in English, so you write it in your first language.

_____ **5.** You ask a friend to help you express an idea in writing.

_____ **6.** You don't know how to spell a word, so you make a guess.

_____ **7.** You erase several sentences because you feel they don't sound good.

_____ **8.** You begin writing about one topic, but change topics several times.

_____ **9.** You put a star next to an idea you want to write more about later.

_____ **10.** While you are writing, you stop to check some information online.

B. *Compare answers with a partner or in a group. Then discuss them with the class.*

EXERCISE 2

A. *Write your answers to these questions. Think about both your first language and English.*

1. In your life so far, have you done more writing for accuracy, more writing for fluency, or a mix of both? Give some examples.

In your first language (Circle one.) more accuracy / more fluency / both

Examples: _____

_____

In English (Circle one.) more accuracy / more fluency / both

Examples: _____

_____

(continued)

2. This year, what are some types of writing you will do where accuracy is more important? Where fluency is more important?

In your first language

Accuracy writing: _____

_____

Fluency writing: _____

_____

In English

Accuracy writing: _____

_____

Fluency writing: _____

_____

3. In the future, what types of writing do you think you will do? How important are accuracy and fluency to these types of writing?

In your first language _____

_____

In English _____

_____

4. Do you practice writing for fluency on your own now (for example, on a blog or in a journal)?

In your first language yes / no

Examples: _____

_____

In English yes / no

Examples: _____

_____

B. *Compare answers in a group. Then discuss them with the class.*

Keeping a Journal

An excellent way to practice your writing fluency in English is to keep an English journal. A journal is a notebook or a computer document where you can write your thoughts and ideas freely. Some people use a journal like a diary—to record their experiences or thoughts throughout the day or week. Others use their journals to describe travel adventures or dreams, or to write stories and poems.

There are many types of journals. You can even draw pictures, add photos or quotes, or include articles from the newspaper. Your journal should reflect who you are and how you think.

In your journal, you might write responses to questions or topics assigned by your teacher, or you might choose your own topics to write about. You can write in your journal daily, weekly, or as assigned by your teacher. The important thing is to write regularly.

Since the goal of journal writing is to increase your fluency, your teacher will not grade your journal on accuracy features, such as grammar, vocabulary, or spelling. However, you may be graded on whether you complete your journal on time, whether you followed the assignment correctly, the number of entries, or (in some cases) the length of the entries.

Warm Up

Work in a group. Discuss these questions:

- What are some reasons that people keep a journal?
- Have you ever kept a journal in your first language, or do you keep one now?
  - If yes, what kinds of things did / do you write about?
  - If no, what kinds of things do you think you would enjoy writing about?
- What are some reasons to keep a journal in a foreign language?

TYPES OF JOURNALS

Here are some common types of journals used in writing classes. The main purpose of all these types of journals is to give you practice expressing your ideas freely in writing.

1. **Freewriting Journals:** Students write in a notebook or on a computer document. They write freely about a topic (or topics) they choose. The journals are not corrected for spelling or grammar.

2. **Guided Response Journals:** Students write on a given topic or answer a specific question. These can be assigned by the teacher or brainstormed by the class.

3. **Diaries:** Students write about what they did during the day (or week). They list events and describe their feelings and reactions.

4. **Dialogue (Partner) Journals:** This type of journal is a kind of "conversation on paper." Students write about a topic of their choice, and then the teacher or another student responds to the journal entry, making comments or asking questions. The next time, the student responds to comments and responses, and so on. This type of writing can even be done by email with a partner in another classroom (or country!).

For this class, your teacher may choose to use one journal type, or he or she may give you different types of journal assignments at different times during the course.

EXERCISE 1

A. *Read these journal samples from students in a writing class. Circle the type of journal.*

1. freewriting / guided response / diary / dialogue

> Today I want to write about the challenge of working and studying at the same time. Before I came here, I never thought about this topic. In my country, almost all students are full time. In my country, we think the ~~job~~ work of being a student is a full-time job! I was very surprised that my roommate works 15 hours a week. She works in the library on campus, so she says she can ~~stay~~ study there when it isn't busy. There are other jobs on campus that are ~~ever~~ even busier. Some students also have jobs off campus, like in restaurants or stores. I don't see how they can do their homework and still have a job. I don't have a job, and I ~~can't still~~ still can't always finish my assignments, especially the reading. I think the cost of university here is too high. That's why people have to work at the same time. I guess it's good to get some work experience at the same time, though. Maybe it's easier to get a job after graduating because of that.

2. freewriting / guided response / diary / dialogue

Journal Assignment
May 10
Q: For you, what is the most challenging thing about writing? Why?

A: For me, I think the most challenging part is organizing my ideas. Before, I thought it was difficult to find many good ideas. But after practicing brainstorming in this class, it has become a lot easier for me. ~~At first, I~~ However, after I get a lot of ideas, it's still hard for me to decide which ones to use, and what order to put them in. ~~I don't know how~~ I'm not sure what the best solution is. Maybe I will try a different kind of brainstorming, like a word map. That way I can see connections. Another idea is to talk to some classmates after I brainstorm but before I write my outline. If I discuss my ideas, it might help me to get more organized. On my last paper, my grade for organization was not so good. So I think this is the best area for me to work on now. If I organize my ideas well before I write, then my paper will be more organized when I write it.

3. freewriting / guided response / diary / dialogue

This week was a good week. Monday was a holiday, so I went to the lake with my roommate and two of his friends. We had a picnic. We wanted to rent boats, but we didn't have enough money. So we just walked around a bit and ate lunch. My classes were easy this week, too. In my hardest class (history) we watched an interesting film. We didn't have to do an assignment afterward, we just talked about it in class. Yesterday was my friend's birthday, so we had a small party at her apartment. Everyone brought some food, like pizza or chips. Someone brought a lot of DVDs to watch, but we had such a good time talking that we never watched a movie. Next week I have several major tests, so I'm really glad this week was relaxing.

(continued)

4. freewriting / guided response / diary / dialogue

September 30

Hi Sanjay.

In the last journal entry, you asked about my family. I have one older brother and one younger sister. My older brother is married, and he lives in a different city, so I don't see him very often. We are connected on Facebook, so I can still see what he is doing. He often posts pictures of his baby. My sister is still in high school. She is very active and has a lot of friends, but she and I are not so close, so I don't talk to her that much. I would like to tell her to be more serious about her high school studies because now I know how hard college can be, but I don't feel close enough to her to say things like that. How about you? Do you have brothers and sisters? Do they live near you?

October 6

Dear Patrice,

I have one older sister who lives in Montreal—she married a Canadian. I've only been there once to visit her, but we had a great time. I read an interesting article in a blog last week about birth order and its effect on personality. Have you heard about this before? The theory is that whether you are the oldest, middle, or youngest child has an influence on your personality and behavior. For example, a middle child (like you) is . . .

B. *Work with another student. Discuss these questions:*

- Which journal entry do you think took the least amount of time to write? Which took the most amount of time? Why?

- Which entry do you think took the most planning before writing it? Which took the least?

- Can you guess what each writer might write about next time?

A. *Practice each type of journal on a separate piece of paper. (You will share your writing with other students.) For your first entry, freewrite for five minutes on any topic of your choice.*

Notes:

When you freewrite . . .

• Keep writing. Don't stop until you've reached the time limit.

• Write freely. Quickly write what comes to your mind about the topic.

• Don't worry about how it sounds.

• Don't pay a lot of attention to grammar, spelling, or punctuation.

B. *Practice a guided response journal entry. Choose one of these topics. Write for five minutes about the topic.*

• A time when you felt proud
• A favorite place
• A movie you disliked
• Rain days

C. *Practice a diary journal entry. Choose one day from the past week. Write for five minutes about that day. Describe the events of the day, as well as your thoughts, feelings, and reactions.*

D. *Practice a dialogue journal entry. Work with another student. Follow these steps:*

1. Write for two or three minutes to your partner. Tell him or her about something, or ask him or her some questions.
2. Exchange papers and read your partner's entry.
3. Write a response to your partner for about three minutes.
4. Exchange papers again.

E. *Work in a group. Answer these questions about the practice journal entries:*

• Which of your journal entries is longest? Which is shortest?
• Which type was most interesting for you? Why?
• Which was easiest to write? Which was the most challenging? Why?

A. *How should your class do journals? Complete the questionnaire about your journal preferences. Check (✓) the appropriate columns.*

	Agree	Not Sure / It Depends	Disagree
1. I want to write in my journal during class.			
2. I want to write in my journal at home.			
3. I want the teacher to read my journal.			
4. I want my classmates to read my journal.			
5. I want to write in a notebook for my journal.			
6. I want to use a computer to write my journal.			
7. I want the teacher to choose the journal topics or questions.			
8. I want to write my own list of topics or questions.			
9. I want to write freely, without a certain topic.			
10. I want to write only once a week.			
11. I want to write several times a week.			
12. I want to receive a grade for my journal.			
13. I want my teacher to give me a time limit for my writing.			
14. I want my teacher to tell me how many pages to write.			
15. Which types of journals are you most interested in doing? (Circle one or more.)	Dialogue Diary	Freewriting Guided Response	

B. *Work in a group. Discuss your responses. Then share your ideas with the class.*

YOUR CLASS JOURNAL

To help you work on your writing fluency, keep an English journal throughout this course. Your teacher may assign journal topics weekly or more or less frequently. You can also use your journal on your own to write down your thoughts, ideas, new words in English, lists of things you want to remember to do, or even to freewrite when you are riding on the train or bus.

EXERCISE 4

Discuss these questions with your teacher and your whole class, and write the answers.

1. Will your journal be done in a notebook or on the computer? _____

2. How often will you write in your journal? _____

3. About how long (time and length) should an entry be? _____

4. Will you write in your journal in class, at home, or both? _____

5. Will your teacher assign the topics, or will you choose them, or both? _____

6. Which type(s) of journal (diary, dialogue, etc.) will you do? _____

7. Will anyone read your journal? Who? _____

Journal Topic Ideas

Here are some journal topic ideas to help you and your class get started with keeping a journal:

- Describe your best friend.

- Explain a good way to have fun.

- Write about your favorite kind of music or a song you like.

- Write about a difficult decision you had to make.

- Describe your favorite movie or book.

- What is the last thing you bought? How did you choose it?

- Describe a time you felt . . . angry, shy, confident, sad, frightened, happy, selfish, lonely, nervous, etc.

- Write about a favorite place.

- Write about a member of your family.

- Write about a dish that you like to cook.

- What interested you the most in class this week? What else would you like to know about that topic?

- Describe a holiday you enjoy / don't enjoy.

(continued)

- What is a talent you wish you had? Why?

- What was the best thing that happened to you this week?

- Write about a memory from your childhood.

- Is there anything in your studies at the moment that seems challenging to you? What are some ways that you can meet that challenge?

- What is something popular that you don't like?

- Describe the qualities of a good parent, teacher, friend, student, or employee.

- What is your favorite kind of weather? Why? What activities do you like to do in that kind of weather?

- Why are you learning English?

- What are some things you miss about your country?

- Write about someone you admire.

- What is your favorite website? Why do you like it?

- Write your thoughts about one of these topics: trees, rain, traffic, the moon, shoes, cell phones, texting, jokes, bears, jewelry, the color blue, silence.

UNIT 2

Blogging

The word *blog* comes from *Web log*, meaning an online journal that is usually written by one person or a small group of people. Often blogs feature writers' personal opinions about one or more topics. Blogs can be shared just among friends or family members. However, many blogs are available to the public and may have thousands or even millions of readers. Blogs are so popular now that new English words have even been introduced to talk about them, such as a *blogger* (a person who writes a blog) and *to blog / blogging* (the process of writing a blog or a blog entry, also called a *blog post* or *posting*).

For this course, your teacher can make a class blog for you and your classmates to use at **http://pearsonELT.com/writingpowerblog**. On the blog, you and your classmates can practice posting on topics that interest you. You will be able to read each other's posts and make comments on them. See the Introduction to this book for more on how to get started on your *Writing Power 3* class blog.

After some practice on your class blog, you can set up your own blog. This unit will help you think about and plan the topics and features of your blog.

Warm Up

Work in a group. Discuss these questions:

- What are some blogs you have seen or visited? If you don't remember the titles, describe the content.

- How did you find those blogs?

- Are there any blogs you read regularly? If so, describe them.

- Do you write (or have you ever written) a blog? If so, what is / was it about?

- If you haven't visited or written a blog before, explain why not. What kinds of topics are you interested in reading or writing about on a blog?

BLOG TOPICS

What do bloggers blog about? Just about everything, from their own lives, careers, and hobbies to topics of local, national, and international importance. There are blogs about art, books, cooking, fitness, health, news, music, travel, soccer, photography—if you can think of a topic, there is probably a blog about it.

Some bloggers post only their own thoughts, and some include information (including photos and videos) from other sites.

EXERCISE 1

A. *Complete the survey about your blog interests. Check (✓) the appropriate columns.*

How interested would you be in reading a blog . . .	Very Interested	Somewhat Interested	Not Interested
1. by a friend or family member?	○	○	○
2. by someone famous?	○	○	○
3. about a stranger's personal life?	○	○	○
4. about events in your local community?	○	○	○
5. about national politics or events?	○	○	○
6. about international politics or events?	○	○	○
7. about sports? (If interested, which sports? _____)	○	○	○
8. about food, exercise, or health?	○	○	○
9. about music, movies, or entertainment?	○	○	○
10. about pets or animals?	○	○	○
11. about another topic? (What topic? _____)	○	○	○
12. that includes photos?	○	○	○
13. that includes videos?	○	○	○
14. that allows readers to post comments?	○	○	○

B. *Work with another student. Share your survey responses. Explain your choices.*

A. *Label each blog post with a blog type from the box. (There is one extra type.)*

> Personal / Diary blog   Travel and Culture blog   Review blog
> Fashion and Lifestyle blog   How-To / Tutorial blog   Class blog

1. _____

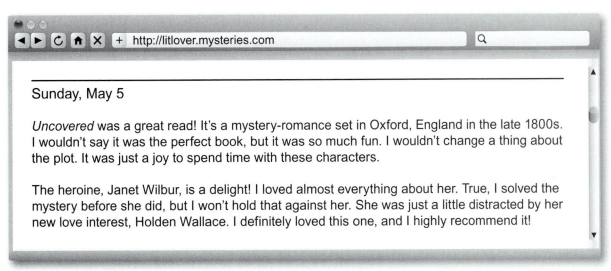

http://litlover.mysteries.com

Sunday, May 5

Uncovered was a great read! It's a mystery-romance set in Oxford, England in the late 1800s. I wouldn't say it was the perfect book, but it was so much fun. I wouldn't change a thing about the plot. It was just a joy to spend time with these characters.

The heroine, Janet Wilbur, is a delight! I loved almost everything about her. True, I solved the mystery before she did, but I won't hold that against her. She was just a little distracted by her new love interest, Holden Wallace. I definitely loved this one, and I highly recommend it!

2. _____

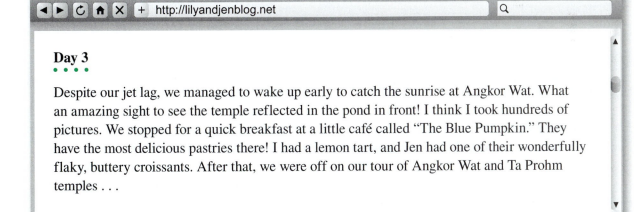

http://lilyandjenblog.net

Day 3

Despite our jet lag, we managed to wake up early to catch the sunrise at Angkor Wat. What an amazing sight to see the temple reflected in the pond in front! I think I took hundreds of pictures. We stopped for a quick breakfast at a little café called "The Blue Pumpkin." They have the most delicious pastries there! I had a lemon tart, and Jen had one of their wonderfully flaky, buttery croissants. After that, we were off on our tour of Angkor Wat and Ta Prohm temples . . .

(continued)

3. _____

JANUARY 17

Sorry I haven't posted anything for a few weeks. I got busy with final exams, and then I was looking for a job—searching online, sending out résumés, going to interviews. It's a lot of work! I think I finally found a job, though. I had an excellent interview with an organization that helps find homes for stray animals. My interview was on Thursday, and there was a message from the manager on my voicemail when I got home from the movies on Friday night. It was too late to call back, so now I have to wait until Monday . . .

4. _____

A lot of people have been writing and asking about the paper lamps in the photos I posted last week. I learned to make those at a great workshop I attended last summer. They aren't really easy, but with a little practice (and some patience), you can make these beautiful, decorative lampshades. You'll need the following materials: 10 sheets of colored paper, clear tape . . .

5. _____

Posted by Sung Min

Yesterday's field trip to the science museum was great! We visited the butterfly garden, where live butterflies were flying all around us. My favorite exhibit was probably "Planets and Stars." We learned about how stars are "born" and "die" and how long it takes the light from a star to reach Earth.

Posted by Luis

I learned a lot on our trip to the Museum of Science. We saw a presentation called "Catching the Wind" about how wind can be used to make electricity . . .

B. *Look again at the survey on page 14. Think about the kind of blog you would like to write. Then discuss these questions:*

- What kinds of topics would you write about?

- What types of features would you include on your blog?

EXERCISE 3

Work with a partner. Look at each blog page. For each blog, discuss these questions:

- What is your first impression of each blog page? Comment on the overall "look and feel" (title, photos, organization, etc.).

- What can you tell about each of the bloggers (personality, interests, writing style, etc.)?

- Which blog would you be most likely to read regularly? Why?

Blog 1—page 1

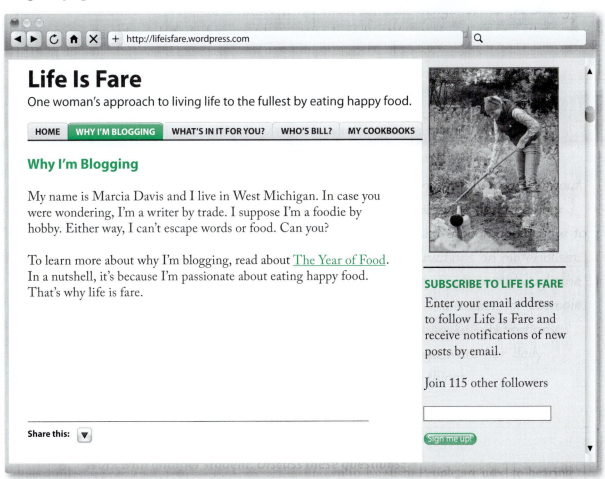

(continued)

http://lifeisfare.wordpress.com/2010/07/26/the-latest-culinary-obsession-foraging

The Latest Culinary Obsession: Foraging   +

Life is Fare
The Latest Culinary Obsession: Foraging
Posted on July 26, 2012 | 122 Comments

Foraging—the act of looking or searching for food—is what humans used to do to survive before agriculture was introduced.

Now, foraging is the new trend in the culinary world. In fact, searching woods, parks, or even cracks in the pavement for edible plants has become the latest culinary obsession, according to an article in this week's issue of *Yum* magazine.

In San Francisco, one organization hosts a monthly "underground market" where you can taste and purchase food that is being produced in backyards and home kitchens in the Bay Area.

A restaurant in Los Angeles called Forage lets people bring in stuff they find in exchange for credit toward dinner.

Two cookbooks on foraging are coming out this fall: *Noma* by Rene Redzepi and *The Wild Table* by forager Connie Green from Northern California.

What do you have growing in your backyard and in the woods near you? If you want to give it a try, check out Foraging.com for resources to help you find edible plants where you live.

122 Responses So Far

Igor27 | July 26, 2012 at 5:38 pm | Reply
There are lots of edible plants that grow in my area. I'd really like to learn some recipes for how to make them taste better!

Marcia Davis | July 26, 2012 at 6:30 pm | Reply
I am a complete novice, Igor! I would love to learn more! I don't mind the cooking, as long as I don't die from choosing the wrong plant!

Igor27 | July 26, 2012 at 8:30 pm | Reply
For wild greens, one thing that works is adding salt and butter. Lots and lots of butter, lol.

Marcia Davis | July 26, 2012 at 9:04 pm | Reply
Great tip, Igor. Thanks for stopping by!

BobandEllen | July 27, 2012 at 11:59 am | Reply
Brilliant ideas!

Blog 2

http://betsyrodman.wordpress.com

B-Mused
Musings by Betsy

About Me

Critters of the New Mexico Desert

Day 2: Last night, our first night here in New Mexico, there was a full moon. Soon after we went to bed, we heard the dramatic howlings of a LARGE coyote pack, uncomfortably nearby. Quite an eerie sound if you've never heard it. We've heard them almost every night while here, sometimes so close to the house that you can hear their feet padding in the grass outside the windows. One night I even got up and closed the glass door, just in case they could figure out how to open the screen. (Just kidding—sort of.) Interestingly enough, the dogs get REALLY quiet when the coyotes are around.

Day 5: OK. So mom sends me out to pick peaches from her tree which is COVERED with these REALLY scary looking large black wasp-like insects with bright red wings (about 5 cm long). She claims they supposedly (ahem!) don't sting, or at least are not aggressive. Watching me try to pick around these critters must have been like a comedy show. (Seriously—I kept thinking there MUST be a hidden camera somewhere.) I would circle the tree, scanning for peaches with no bugs on them. I would cautiously creep in toward the branch, eyes scanning wildly for the winged monsters, grab a peach then run, making sure nothing was chasing me. To my credit, I did this until my bowl was full, as instructed. What a good daughter, eh? I did some research to identify this insect. It is the New Mexico state insect, the tarantula hawk, named for its skill in hunting tarantulas, which it feeds to its young underground. The adults only eat nectar, fruit, and pollen. It turns out this beast has one of the most painful stings in the insect world. Here's a quote from Bug-o-Pedia.com: *The tarantula hawk rarely stings unless it is provoked. The sting is one of the most painful of any insect, but the terrible pain only lasts for about 3 minutes.*

15 Responses to "Critters of the New Mexico Desert"

Susanna Says:
August 10, 2012 at 2:17 pm
Wow! What a wonderful collection!

Anna68 Says:
August 15, 2012 at 12:13 pm
I hope those were the best peaches you ever ate! I am so glad you didn't have 3 minutes of terrible pain to get them, but just the risk of it is enough!

Betsy Says:
August 15, 2012 at 1:52 pm
Seriously—I'll never let my mother forget it. (The pie WAS delicious, though!)

A BLOG OF YOUR OWN

You and your classmates can use the **Writing Power Blog** (http://pearsonELT.com/writingpowerblog) to practice blog posts throughout this course, or for a time period set by your teacher. (See page vi for more information.)

When you are comfortable with blogging, you can try creating a blog of your own. There are many free Internet websites where you can set up a blog easily.

Your blog can include information about you and why you're blogging. It can be a personal journal or diary blog, or another type (How-to blog, Review blog, Fashion and Lifestyle blog, etc.). Your teacher will help you decide on topics to write about. You can keep your own personal blog, or you can share your blog with a partner if you have the same interests, as long as both of you post.

A. *Use this idea web to plan your own blog. Add as many ideas as you can.*

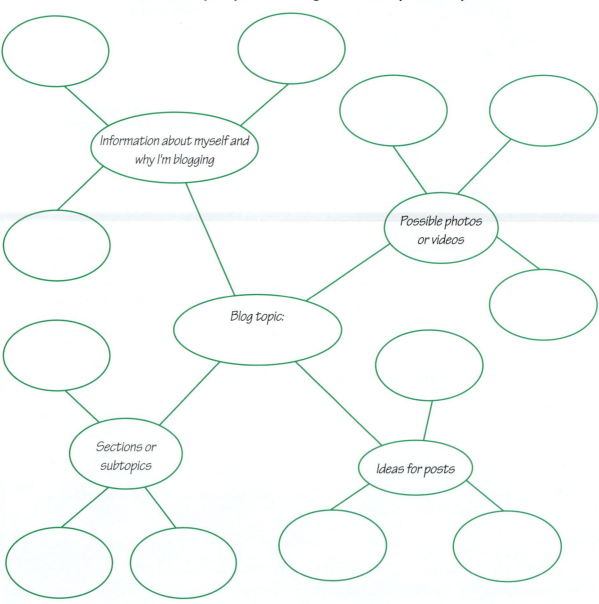

B. *Work with another student. Share your idea webs. Make suggestions for what to include on each other's blogs.*

C. *Discuss these questions with your teacher and your class. Write the answers.*

1. How often should you post on your blog? _____

2. About how long (how many words) should each post be? _____

3. Should you be required to read classmates' blogs? If so, how many and how often?

_____

Are you also required to leave comments? _____

4. What additional rules or guidelines should there be for the blog? _____

_____

_____

5. What will your first post be about? _____

_____

UNIT 3

Creative Writing

Creative writing is a good way to challenge yourself and "stretch your writing muscles." Some students say that creative writing in English gives them the freedom to express themselves in ways they can't in their first language.

There is no right way or wrong way when it comes to creative writing. This kind of writing will expand your vocabulary and storytelling abilities, both important elements of good writing.

You may even surprise yourself and discover a hidden talent. Whether you feel you are "creative" or not, the exercises in this unit will help you develop skills for more detailed, fuller expression in your writing.

Warm Up

Work in a group. Discuss these questions:

- What does the word *creative* mean to you? Do you think you are creative?

- Is creativity something you are born with, or something you learn, or a little of both?

- What are some examples of creative writing?

- How can practicing creative writing help you become a better writer in general?

DESCRIPTION AND SENSORY DETAILS

Good writers are able to describe people, places, feelings, objects, and situations in detail.

Writers use a variety of techniques to make their descriptions come to life on the page. They may compare and contrast people or objects, or use descriptive details to capture the reader's interest, emotions, and imagination.

Sensory details describe the way something smells, feels, looks, sounds, or tastes. Including these types of descriptions is a powerful way to bring your writing to life. Good writers use sensory details whenever possible.

EXERCISE 1

A. *Read the short passage, "Peter's Beach," by Caleb Gattegno. How does the passage make you feel?*

B. *How many of the five senses (sight, hearing, touch, taste, smell) does the writer include descriptions for? Which ones are they?*

Peter's Beach

In front of the house there was a beach. Peter liked to stretch on the sand when the sun was warming it. From the back door of the house he would walk along a path as far as the sand, and stand at the water's edge looking at the sea. When nothing very interesting was happening on the water, he would go down on his knees and take a handful of sand. Through his fingers ran the sand till only small stones and shells were left. Then with a large sweep of his arm and with as much strength as he could muster Peter would throw them away as far as he could.

At other times he would go on his back and gaze up at the clouds, his hands idly searching the sand at his sides. He never stopped playing with the sand and feeling it run through his fingers, however much he was absorbed by the changes in the clouds.

Occasionally some fishing boats came close enough to the beach for Peter to see what the fishermen were doing. Then with his hands clasped he would look and look, while his whole body moved with the boat from side to side. When the fishermen drew in their nets or cast them into the water, Peter would do the same with an imaginary net of his own from his place on the beach.

On the small beach Peter had a place of his own.

C. *Work with another student. Discuss these questions. Write your answers.*

1. What does Peter see on his beach?

   _____

2. What sensations does Peter feel?

   _____

3. In addition to the sights and sensations the writer describes, what else do you think Peter . . .

   sees?   _____

   hears? _____

   feels? _____

   smells? _____

4. What emotions do you think Peter is feeling? Why do you think so? _____

   _____

EXERCISE 2

A. *Think about a familiar place you visit often. Choose from one of the following places, or use your own idea:*

- a park or a garden
- a restaurant or a café
- a lake, pond, or river
- a neighborhood in your city or town
- a friend's home

- a mountain
- a relative's kitchen
- a forest
- a shopping mall or store

B. *Imagine you are at the place now. Read these questions. Then close your eyes for one minute and imagine the place.*
- Are you alone? If you are with someone, who is it? What does the person look like?
- What are you doing? Are you sitting, walking, talking?
- What do you see around you? What sights, shapes, colors?
- What sounds can you hear? What do they sound like?
- What do you smell?
- What sensations do you feel? (Do you feel hot, warm, cool? Are you comfortable?)
- How do you feel in this environment? (What emotions?)

C. *Make some notes to answer each question. Then do a ten-minute freewrite about the place. Describe the sights, sounds, smells, and feelings in detail.*

D. *Compare your writing with another student. How is it the same? How is it different?*

E. *Complete the chart with useful words and phrases you and your partner used to describe sensory details.*

Sight	Sounds	Feeling (Touch)	Taste	Smell

A DIFFERENT PERSPECTIVE

Another technique, often used by creative writers, is to look at things from a different perspective, or point of view. This involves imagining and writing about the way someone else—or something else—might think, feel, or react in a situation. Looking at people, places, and things from different perspectives has given the world some of its greatest masterpieces.

EXERCISE 3

A. *Read the passage. Who or what is telling the story? Compare your idea with another student. Discuss the reasons for your answer.*

Why did they put me in this cold, dark corner of the room? Don't they know I need the light of the sun? Without it, I'll die! Each day, I watch through the window across the room. I see the sun move slowly across the yard until it disappears behind the hill. Then the long, dark shadows fold in around me again. I am alone watching the world pass me by. Outside I can see so many tall trees with their thick, strong arms reaching for the sky. The sunlight warms their branches, and the wind makes their leaves dance. They are never lonely. They have visits from furry gray squirrels and happy, singing birds building their nests. I wish I could escape from this dry pot of dirt and join them!

B. *Look back at the passage. Underline the sensory details the writer included. Then compare your work with another student.*

A. *Choose three of these ideas. Imagine you are the main character in each. Do a five-minute freewrite from each perspective.*

- You are the chairs in a dining room. There is a dinner party going on. Describe the event from the chairs' perspective.

- You are a book on a library shelf. A person near the shelf is looking for a book to read. Write about the scene from the book's perspective.

- You are the only small child attending an adult's birthday party.

- You are a computer and you have been invaded by a virus.

- You are a parent at your child's wedding.

- You are the teacher in this class.

- You are a seashell on the beach.

- You are the sun or the moon.

- You are a bird in a cage.

- You are a thunderstorm cloud.

- You are the wind.

B. *Read your freewrites. Choose the one you like best and develop it into a short composition (two to three paragraphs) from the main character's perspective. Include as many sensory details as you can.*

STORY PROMPTS

Many fiction writers use writing prompts or pictures to help get their stories started. This section includes some common types of activities used by teachers of creative writing.

Story Chains

A story chain is a popular creative writing activity. One person begins writing the story and then passes it to the next person who continues the story. The last person in the group ends the story. No one can predict how the story will unfold. The writing is truly spontaneous and full of surprises.

A. ***Work in a group of four. Follow the instructions to write a story.***

    1. Look at the four story prompts.

    2. Assign one story prompt to each person in the group.

    3. Each person starts writing his or her story on a clean piece of paper. Write for five minutes. Include the phrases from the story prompt.

    4. After five minutes, each person passes his or her paper to the person on the right.

    5. The next person continues the story and writes for five more minutes.

    6. Repeat steps 4 and 5 until each person has written on each paper once.

    Story Prompt 1

        a woman named Helena; a letter

    Story Prompt 2

        a couple in a car; a dark, stormy night

    Story Prompt 3

        a man, a woman, and a child; a deserted island

    Story Prompt 4

        a person; money on the sidewalk

B. ***Take turns reading the completed stories aloud. Then with your group, choose one story to share with the class.***

Picture Stories

Do you know the expression, "A picture is worth a thousand words?" It's very true when it comes to creative writing. Through the years, great writers have been inspired to develop fascinating and entertaining stories from paintings and photographs. Some famous examples include *Girl with the Pearl Earring*, a book and film based on a painting by the Dutch artist Vermeer, or *Sunday in the Park with George*, a Broadway musical based on the painting *A Sunday Afternoon on the Island of La Grande Jatte* by French painter Georges Seurat.

A. **Look at the pictures. Think about these questions:**
  • Describe the situations. What's happening?
  • What do you think was happening before the picture was taken?
  • What do you think happened after the picture was taken?
  • Think about the details and descriptions you will include.

B. **Choose one picture to write about. Write a short story (four or five paragraphs) from the perspective of one of the characters in the picture. Include answers to the questions in Exercise A and as many sensory details as you can.**

C. **Work with another student. Take turns reading your stories aloud. Then discuss these questions with the class:**
  • What did you like about your partner's story?
  • What details surprised you or moved you?
  • What descriptions helped make the characters or setting real?

Further Practice

Journal or Blog Topics

Use your journal or blog to continue your creative writing practice. Here are some ideas for creative writing activities:

- Write a story that begins with this sentence: *It was a day I'll never forget . . .*
- Write a story that uses all of these words: *elevator, purse, flower, string, chewing gum.*
- Write a story from the perspective of a young boy's shoes.
- Write a creative excuse to your teacher about why you didn't do your homework.
- Write a story from the perspective of a baby learning to walk.
- Write a story that begins with this sentence: *Once upon a time, there lived a poor young girl with a surprising ability . . .*
- Write a story from the perspective of a pet goldfish.
- Write an announcement to the world about your wonderful new invention to improve people's lives. Find an interesting photo or picture—your own or one from a magazine or the Internet. Use it to write a story or a dialogue.

Language Use

Introduction

In this part of *Writing Power 3,* you will work on developing language skills for writing in many different situations—how to build a rich vocabulary to draw upon for your writing, and how to write sentences and paragraphs in English that are correct and that effectively communicate the ideas, information, and feelings you want to express. These units will help your English sound more natural and more interesting.

Skills introduced in Part 2 include:

- Vocabulary Building
- Sentence Variety
- Relating Ideas
- Verbs: Tense and Voice
- Figurative Language

Good Paragraphs: A Review

You have probably studied writing paragraphs before, and you will learn more about different patterns for organizing paragraphs in Part 3.

However, for many of the assignments in Part 2, you will need to write good paragraphs. Please review these guidelines with your teacher.

Guidelines for Good Paragraphs

Indented First Line

Usually the first line of a new paragraph is indented—placed slightly to the right of the rest of the text.

> ***Example:***
>
> →*Xxxx xxx x xx xxxxx. Xxx xxx xxxxxxx x xx? Xx xxxxxx xx xxx xxxx xxxx x. Xxxxxxx xx x xxxx. Xx xxx xxxxx xx xx x. X xxxxx xxxx xx xxxxxxxxx xx xxxxx.*

One Topic and One Main Idea

Good paragraphs are about one topic and one main idea. All paragraphs include a topic sentence.

- The topic is the broad subject—what the paragraph is about.
- The main idea is usually the writer's feeling or opinion about the topic.
- The topic sentence is usually the first sentence in a paragraph. It introduces the topic and gives the main idea.

Examples:

> Topic: *my grandmother*
> Main Idea: *taught me the meaning of giving*
> Topic Sentence: *It was my grandmother who taught me the true meaning of giving.*

Supporting Sentences and Details

Supporting points are all the other sentences in the paragraph that develop the main idea. Details can be examples, explanations, or descriptions that add to the supporting points.

Examples:

- Supporting Point 1

  My grandmother's door was always open to visitors. Whenever she cooked, she always made extra food. She felt it was important to always be ready to offer a home-cooked meal to anyone who stopped by.

- Supporting Point 2

  In addition, my grandmother helped others by volunteering at a hospital. She delivered flowers or mail to patients and helped them with things they could not do for themselves, like writing letters, for example.

- Supporting Point 3

  Furthermore, even though my grandmother was a very busy woman, she always had time for me. I'll never forget the many books she read to me or games she played with me when I was a child.

Conclusion

The last sentence or two of the paragraph summarizes the main idea or the opinion of the writer.

Example:

> *Finally, my grandmother never told me what I should or should not do. She didn't need to. She was a living example.*

If you follow these general rules, you will be able to write successful, well-organized paragraphs.

Vocabulary Building

With the right words, you can express exactly what you want to convey. Building a rich vocabulary will give your writing variety and make it sound more natural. You have already learned many words as you have worked toward becoming a more fluent writer in English.

In this unit, you will learn and practice strategies for finding the right vocabulary, as well as ways of collecting and reviewing vocabulary to improve your writing.

These strategies include:

- Selecting useful words
- Keeping a vocabulary notebook
- Reviewing with flash cards

You'll also learn the following ways to expand your vocabulary:

- Focusing on word families
- Learning synonyms and antonyms
- Studying collocations and phrases

Using these strategies will help you better understand information and decide which new words will be useful for your writing.

Note: For this unit and the rest of this course, you will need a vocabulary notebook. You will use this notebook for keeping useful words you can use for your writing.

Warm Up

A. *Take this vocabulary learning quiz. Read the statements and write* T *(true) or* F *(false).*

_____ 1. Reading in English is one of the best ways to build vocabulary.

_____ 2. It's important to look up every new word in the dictionary.

_____ 3. Writing a word helps you remember it.

_____ 4. To really learn a new word, you need to see / hear / read / use it several times.

_____ 5. You can find a list of the most useful words in English.

B. *Compare answers with another student. Check the answers on page 47. Then discuss these questions:*

- How often do you read in English? When and what kinds of things do you read?
- What do you do when you find a new word in something you are reading?
- How do you decide which words to look up in the dictionary?
- Do you already have a special place, like a notebook, to keep new vocabulary?

SELECTING USEFUL WORDS

One of the best ways to build your English vocabulary is by reading in English. You will find new and useful words when you read a textbook, article, or book. As you know, understanding new words and expressions is often necessary for understanding information.

How Do You Know Which Words Are Useful for Your Writing?

- When you read, words and expressions that are important are often **repeated in the text**, or **used to describe or explain** an aspect of the topic.

- Words or phrases that **you hear and see often** and in many different types of texts are probably useful. This means that they are used frequently about many different topics.

- Words and phrases that **relate to your own studies, work, or personal interests** will probably be useful for you to learn.

- You can also use a **word list** to find out if a word is common or useful. In the Appendix, you will find a list of the 3,000 words used most frequently in academic writing. There are also lists of frequently used words in English in some dictionaries and on the Internet.

Guidelines for Selecting Useful Words

To decide whether a word will be useful for your writing, ask yourself these questions:

- Have I seen the word before?

- Is the word repeated in the text?

- Does the word relate to, describe, or explain an aspect of the topic?

- Is the word related to my studies, work, or personal interests?

- Is it on a frequently used word list?

If you answer *yes* to two or more of the questions, the word is probably useful for you. Write it in your vocabulary notebook, look it up, and write the definitions. Then study it along with other new words.

Read the following passages. Follow these instructions for each passage:

1. Write the topic.
2. Circle any words you <u>know</u> that relate to the topic.
3. Underline any words or phrases that are <u>new</u> to you. Check them on the word list in the Appendix. Below the passage, write the words you find on the list.
4. Ask yourself the Guidelines questions on page 35 to decide which words and phrases are useful to learn. Write them.

Passage 1

> Physical fitness was never a priority for me. I had not enjoyed playing sports before, and after the first volleyball practice, I had had enough. The practice was strenuous and tedious, and I complained bitterly about it afterward.

Topic: _____

Words on word list: _____

Useful words for my writing: _____

Passage 2

> In one area of psychology, theorists study personality by classifying different personality types. For example, people may be classified as introverts or extroverts. Others may be described as having a type A or type B personality.

Type A Characteristics	Type B Characteristics
• goal-driven	• laidback, easygoing
• overwhelmed and anxious when completing multiple tasks	• do not get stressed
• competitive, must win	• may leave finishing tasks to the last minute
• overachievers	• reflective
• impatient	• steady workers
• often stressed	
• unable to relax, feel they need to get things done	

Topic: _____

Words on word list: _____

Useful words for my writing: _____

Passage 3

> Some of my fondest childhood memories are of the times I was allowed to go outside after dinner in the winter. I would walk out into the solitary dark night, and play in the glittering, white snow. I would make snow angels, climb enormous, steep, snow banks, and revel in the way the snow enveloped me in a comforting, protective embrace. I see why nature is often referred to as "Mother Nature." Her velvety blanket of snow felt solacing, close and safe—all things an infant feels, snuggled in his mother's arms.

Topic: _____

Words on word list: _____

Useful words for my writing: _____

STUDYING NEW WORDS

Now that you know how to select useful words for your writing, you need strategies for how to study and learn them. This section will give you some useful ideas.

Vocabulary Notebooks

Many students keep a special notebook for vocabulary study. It helps them organize and keep track of new words. You can start a vocabulary notebook for writing down useful new words and phrases you encounter in *Writing Power 3* and other sources.

Your vocabulary notebook can be organized alphabetically or by word categories, such as "sports words," "science words," or "school words." It can also include information that will help you understand and remember the words and use them correctly.

Vocabulary notebook entries can include . . .

- the part of speech of the word—noun, verb, adjective, adverb, etc.
- the definition
- the sentence where you found the word
- new sentences with the new word

A. *Start your own vocabulary notebook using the useful vocabulary words you wrote in Exercise 1. Follow these instructions for each word:*

1. On the left side of the page, write the word or phrase.
2. Under the word, write the sentence where you found it.
3. Look up the word in the dictionary.
4. To the right of the word, write its part of speech and definition.
5. Write a new sentence using the word.

Example:

strenuous - adj., using a lot of effort, strength, or determination

"The practice was strenuous and tedious, and I complained bitterly about it afterward."

Moving all the furniture out of my apartment was strenuous work.

B. *Compare notebooks with another student. Did you choose the same useful words?*

Flash Cards

Everyone has his or her own way of memorizing information. For vocabulary, research studies show that in order to learn or remember a new word, you need to see / hear / write / say that word at least seven or eight times over a period of time. One way to memorize your new vocabulary is to set a special time each day to study and review your vocabulary notebook. Another way is to make flash cards.

Flash cards are cards you can use for studying. Your teachers have probably used flash cards to present new English words in class, or they may have used them to teach you math. Flash cards are a great way to quickly review vocabulary on your own or with a partner.

You can make your own cards for the words in your vocabulary notebook. Follow these steps to make flash cards:

1. On the front of the card, write the new word and its part of speech.
2. On the back of the card, write the definition of the word.

Example:

Front   Back

strenuous – adj.   using a lot of effort, strength, or
                                                  determination

A. **Make a flash card for each word in your vocabulary notebook.**

B. **Test yourself with your flash cards. Look at the words and say the definitions. Then look at the definitions and say the words.**

C. **Work with a partner. Exchange flash cards. Take turns testing each other on the words. The person who correctly defines the most words wins.**

D. **Work in a group. Take turns testing each other with your flash cards. Follow these steps:**
    1. One student holds up a flash card.
    2. The next student to the left explains the definition in his or her own words and uses the word in a sentence. (If you are not sure the word has been used correctly in a sentence, ask your teacher.)
    3. If you do not know a word, say, "Pass." Then write it in your vocabulary notebook to study later. Then the next student to the left tries to explain the definition.
    4. The person who defines the most words <u>and</u> uses them correctly in a new sentence wins.

EXPANDING YOUR VOCABULARY

As you continue to build your vocabulary, you will notice that your writing improves. You will have many more words to express your thoughts and ideas. Here are some strategies for expanding your vocabulary.

Word Families

Every word belongs to a word family—words that share the same root. Although words may share the same root and have related meanings, each meaning is a little different.

Look at the forms for the word "compete." Which ones do you know? What are their meanings?

Verb	Noun	Adjective	Adverb
compete	competition	competitive	competitively
	competitor		

When you look up a new word in the dictionary, look at the words before and after it. You may see several related words from the same family.

Example:

compete *v.* to try to win or gain something, or try to be better or more successful than someone else

competition *n.* **1.** a situation in which people or organizations compete with each other; **2.** the people or groups that are competing against you, especially in business; **3.** an organized event in which people or teams compete against each other

competitive *adj.* determined to be more successful than other people or companies

competitively *adv.* in competition

competitor *n.* a person, team, company, etc., that competes against another

In your vocabulary notebook, write down one or more forms of the word you are looking up. That way, you will learn more than just one new word! Learning different word forms will help you build your fluency and increase your ability to write more precisely and accurately.

A. *Work with another student. Complete the chart with as many word forms as you can for each word from this unit. An "X" means no form exists.*

Verb	Noun	Adjective	Adverb
develop			
		steady	
theorize			
			interestingly
	success		
react			X
	research		X

B. *Check your word forms with the class. Write any new words in your vocabulary notebook. Check them in the dictionary and complete the vocabulary notebook entry.*

C. *Make flash cards for each of the new words. Test yourself with a partner. For each word, say the definition and at least one other word in the same word family.*

Synonyms and Antonyms

Learning **synonyms** (words with similar meanings) and **antonyms** (words with opposite meanings) will increase your writing fluency and give your writing variety at the same time.

A word may have many synonyms and antonyms. Each synonym expresses a slightly different aspect or tone of the word. Knowing which one to use will make your writing more precise. Antonyms are also important, especially if you are comparing or contrasting something or need to show the opposite meaning.

Dictionaries often give synonyms and antonyms along with the definitions.

Look at these examples. In the first example, *prohibit* is a synonym for the word *forbid*. The two words have the same meaning. In the second example, *sudden* is the antonym, or opposite, of *gradual*.

for•bid /fɚbɪd/ *v.* to order someone not to do something SYN: **prohibit**

gra•du•al /ɡrædʒuəl/ *adj.* happening, developing, or changing slowly over a long time ANT: **sudden**

Dictionaries and word processing software also often include a *thesaurus*. A thesaurus is a dictionary that lists synonyms and antonyms.

For example, maybe your writing topic is about great inventions. The word *invent* may be needed repeatedly throughout your essay. Look at the thesaurus entry from the *Longman Dictionary of American English* for the word *invent*:

Example:

in•vent /ɪnˈvɛnt/ *v.* [transitive] to make, design, or produce something for the first time [invention, inventor]: • *Who invented the light bulb?*

THESAURUS

create—to invent or design something: • *a dish created by our chef*

think up—to produce an idea, plan, etc., that is completely new: • *Teachers constantly have to think up new ways to keep the kids interested.*

come up with something—to think of a new idea, plan, reply, etc.: • *Carson said he came up with the idea for the book about five years ago.*

devise (formal)—to plan or invent a way of doing something: • *The system was devised as a way of measuring students' progress.*

make up something—to produce a new story, song, game, etc.: • *Grandpa made up stories for us at bedtime.*

dream something up—to think of a plan or idea, especially an unusual one: • *The company's name was dreamed up by Harris's fifteen-year-old daughter.*

EXERCISE 5

A. **Work in a group. Write as many synonyms and antonyms as you can for each listed word in the chart. You may use a dictionary.**

Word	Synonyms	Antonyms
white		
right		

Word	Synonyms	Antonyms
excited		
success		
love		
introverted		
easygoing		

B. **Write any new words in your vocabulary notebook.**

A. *Compare these two passages. Underline the words that are different.*

Passage 1

The sales representative succeeded in selling 100 copies of the newest video game. As a reward, the store's owner gave him a $50 gift certificate. The sales representative was completely surprised. He never thought he would succeed since the game was very expensive.

Passage 2

The sales representative achieved his goal of selling 100 copies of the latest video game. As a bonus, the store's proprietor gave him a $50 gift certificate. The sales representative was completely shocked. He thought he would fail since the game was extremely pricey.

B. *Choose a word you added to the chart in Exercise 5. Write a paragraph of four or five sentences using the word. Include as many synonyms and antonyms for the word as you can. Then share your sentences with the class.*

Collocations and Phrases

Collocations are words that are always used together in a **phrase.** Using collocations will make your writing sound more natural.

The best way to learn collocations is to notice words you often see or hear used together. If you hear or see a phrase several times in different places, it is probably a collocation.

Many learner dictionaries highlight common collocations. Look at the collocations for the word *friend.*

Example:

friend /frɛnd/ *n.* [countable] someone whom you like very much and enjoy spending time with: • *I'm meeting a friend for lunch.* • *Is she a friend of yours?* •*Tony's her best friend.* • *Lee's an old friend.* • *She's one of my closest friends.*

COLLOCATIONS
You may have lots of **good / close friends**, but your **best friend** is the one you like most.

An **old friend** is one you have known for a long time.

If you **have friends**, you know and like them already.

If you **make friends** with someone, you start to know and like them.

Collocation Patterns

Here are some of the most common types of collocations.

Adjective + noun

> It was a **tough decision**.
> a **difficult decision**.
> a **good decision**.

Verb + adverb

> I **didn't feel well**, so I went home early.
> Please **drive carefully**.

Verb + noun

> The mayor **is making a plan** for the new conference center.
> The company **is taking steps** to fix the problem.

Adverb + adjective

> The customer was **completely satisfied**.

EXERCISE 7

A. **Work in a group. Complete the chart with as many of these common verb + noun collocations as you can. Use your dictionary to help you.**

make + noun	take + noun	keep + noun
make a mistake	take a break	keep time

B. **Add any new collocations to your vocabulary notebook.**

Useful Phrases for Academic Writing

Certain set phrases are especially useful for the kinds of writing you may need to do in school. You will find these types of phrases in textbooks and academic articles.

Examples:

The study **showed that** more people are choosing to shop online.

The report **indicated that** most residents were in favor of the change.

The speaker **made the point that** very few people had computers in the past.

According to the article, the research was conducted in June.

A large number of students responded to the survey.

There is **a wide variety of** options available.

In order to save money and energy, the university is turning off computers in the labs.

Companies use the Internet for many forms of advertising, **for instance,** pop-up ads and mass emails. **In addition,** they contact potential customers directly by telephone.

The university has many services, **such as** a tutoring center, a health center, and a career center.

> **Note:** You will learn more about these phrases in Part 3, Academic Writing.

EXERCISE 8

A. **Complete the sentences with phrases from the box.**

according to	for instance	in order to	made the point that
a large number of	in addition	indicated that	such as

1. Products sold online are usually less expensive than products sold in stores. _____, Pellerman Shoes sell for 25 percent less online than in stores.

2. _____ log onto any secure website, you need to create a user name and a password.

3. _____ companies outsource their customer service departments.

4. The survey results _____ one-third of college students use public transportation.

5. The bank offers financial advice to its customers. _____, it offers free checking to anyone who opens a new account.

6. There are several new types of smartphones, _____ the Q series, the *N* series, and the *bT* series.

7. _____ the company's annual report, Thomas Tea is sold in over 20 different countries.

8. The speaker _____ in today's business world, every company should have its own website.

B. *Compare answers with another student. Add any new phrases to your vocabulary notebook.*

EXERCISE 9

A. *Review the new words, collocations, and phrases you added to your vocabulary notebook from this unit. Choose five of them you think are useful for your writing and make flash cards with them.*

B. *Exchange flash cards with another student. Take turns quizzing each other with the cards.*

Answers to Warm Up on page 34

1. T. Reading books is a good way to build your vocabulary because of the number of words you will be exposed to and will see again and again in context.

2. F. It is important, however, to look up words that are necessary for you to understand a text.

3. T. Every time you use the word will help you to remember it.

4. T. Research shows that repeated contact with a new vocabulary word will help you to remember it.

5. T. A number of organizations have researched and published lists of the most frequently used words in English.

UNIT 2

Sentence Variety

It is important for a piece of writing to keep the reader's attention. In addition to including interesting topics or content, the style of writing itself can make a text more or less interesting.

Writers often use the same sentence patterns again and again, creating sentences that are very similar. You can make your writing more interesting by using a variety of sentence types.

In this unit, you will learn ways to add variety to your sentences and paragraphs.

Warm Up

A. ***Work in a group. Look at the pictures. Discuss these questions:***

- Which room do you prefer? Why?

- Which room is most like your own bedroom?

- What kind of person do you think prefers each type of room?

- How often do you go shopping (either online or in a store)? What kinds of things do you buy?

- Do you think you own more things, fewer things, or about the same number of things as a typical person of your age from your country?

B. ***Think about a room in your home. Choose a personal object you have in the room. Write a paragraph describing the object. Where did it come from? What does it mean to you? Keep your paragraph to look at again later in this unit.***

A. *Read and compare the sample paragraphs. Underline the differences in Paragraph 2.*

Paragraph 1

> I read a very interesting book. The book is called *Not Buying It: My Year Without Shopping*. It was written by Judith Levine. It is a personal story. Levine describes her efforts to not buy anything new for one year. It isn't a book about how to stop shopping. It's a book about the author's observations on materialism. She talks about consumerism. She talks about possessions. She talks about conservation. She saved about $8,000. It wasn't easy. She had many challenges. She had to do without some things. She had to make substitutions. The most difficult things for her to change were her daily habits and her attitudes about buying and owning things.

Paragraph 2

> I read a very interesting book called *Not Buying It: My Year Without Shopping*, by Judith Levine. In this personal story, Levine describes her efforts to not buy anything new for one year. It isn't a book about how to stop shopping, but a book about the author's observations on materialism. She talks about consumerism, possessions, and conservation. Although she saved about $8,000, it wasn't easy. She had many challenges; for example, she had to do without some things, and she had to make substitutions. However, the most difficult things for her to change were her daily habits and her attitudes about buying and owning things.

B. *Work with another student. Discuss these questions:*
- What is the same in both paragraphs? What is different?
- Which paragraph do you prefer? Why?

EXPANDING SENTENCES

A paragraph of only short simple sentences might be easy to understand, but it isn't pleasant or interesting to read. It seems boring to the reader. Similarly, a paragraph of only long, complex sentences with many clauses can be difficult to read. A good paragraph includes both short and long sentences.

Expanding Sentences with Prepositional Phrases

One way to vary your writing is to add information to individual sentences. You can often do this with **prepositional phrases**. Prepositional phrases include a preposition—a word such as *at, by, for, from, in, on, with*—and a noun.

Prepositional phrases can function in a sentence as adjectives or adverbs. In these cases, they are called adjective phrases or adverb phrases.

An **adjective phrase** gives more information about a noun by telling what something is like. In the following examples, one-word adjectives are underlined once and adjective phrases are underlined twice.

Examples:

> *I went shopping at the store.*
>
> *I went shopping at the <u>new</u> store <u><u>in the mall</u></u>.*
>
> *The <u>new</u> store <u><u>in the mall</u></u> has <u>lower</u> prices than the <u>fancy</u> boutique <u><u>near my house</u></u>.*

In English, one-word adjectives usually come before the noun, and adjective phrases often come after the noun.

Adverb phrases give more information about the verb, or action in the sentence, by telling *how, why, when,* or *to what degree* something was done. In the following examples, one-word adverbs are underlined once and adverb phrases are underlined twice.

Examples:

> *I go shopping.*
>
> *I <u>usually</u> go shopping <u><u>on weekends</u></u>.*
>
> *I <u>usually</u> go shopping <u><u>with my friends</u></u> <u><u>on weekends</u></u>.*

One-word adverbs usually come directly before or directly after the verb. Note that several adverb phrases can be used in the same sentence. Adverb phrases usually come after the verb, though they often start sentences.

Example:

> *<u><u>On weekends</u></u>, I <u>usually</u> go shopping <u><u>with my friends</u></u>.*

Underline the prepositional phrases in the following sentences. There may be more than one in each sentence.

(1.) I like shopping on the Internet more than shopping in stores. (2.) With my computer, I can shop at all hours. (3.) Also, when I go into a store, I sometimes buy things without really needing them. (4.) For example, last week I went to the department store in my town to buy a pair of shoes for a wedding. (5.) As I walked through the electronics section, I saw a nice alarm clock with a radio. (6.) It was on sale for a really good price, so I bought it. (7.) But I already have an alarm clock with all the features I need, and I have a radio in my bedroom and one in my living room. (8.) So actually, I spent money for something I didn't need, and now I regret it.

Further Practice

Journal or Blog Topic *(See Part 1, Units 1 and 2.)*
- Write a paragraph about a time when you bought something you didn't really need. What made you decide to buy it? How did/do you feel about buying it?

Research and Write
- Ask five students in the class whether they prefer to shop online or in a store. Find out their reasons and take notes on their answers. Then write a paragraph about the results.

A. *Read the paragraph. Then rewrite it on a separate piece of paper. Expand the sentences with one-word adjectives and adverbs, and prepositional phrases.*

I like window shopping. It's almost like going to a museum or a garden. I can look at many items. I don't have to buy them. Just looking at different things is enjoyable. I used to spend money. Now I don't bring my wallet. If I don't have money, I can't spend it.

B. *Compare your work in a group. Take turns reading your paragraphs aloud.*

COMBINING SENTENCES

Another way to add variety to your sentence types is to combine sentences. Here are two common ways.

Coordinating Conjunctions

Coordinating conjunctions are short, useful words that you can use to combine two ideas and to connect two sentences to make one longer one. You can remember this list of seven words with the word "FANBOYS," the first letters of the coordinating conjunctions:

for, and, nor, but, or, yet, and *so*

Example:

I don't think I shop too much.   I have too many things in my apartment.

↓

I don't think I shop too much, **but** *I have too many things in my apartment.*

> **Note:** Use a comma before the coordinating conjunction.
> ### Example:
> *People may say they don't pay attention to ads,* **yet** *they end up buying the products that are advertised most.*

Subordinating Conjunctions

Subordinating conjunctions are words or phrases you can use to express . . .

- time order: *after, as soon as, before, since, when, until*
- cause: *as, because, since*
- contrast: *although, even though, whereas, while*
- condition or reason: *provided that, so that*

Examples:

We had to sell some of our furniture **because** *our house is too small.*

I like to buy souvenirs when I travel **even though** *my room is pretty crowded.*

I'd like to buy a used car **provided that** *I can find a reliable one.*

Notes:

- When the subordinate clause comes second in a sentence, don't use a comma unless you need it for clarity.

   Example:

   We've started selling some of our furniture because our house is too small.

- The subordinate clause can also be placed first. In that case, you must use a comma after the clause.

   Example:

   Because *our house is too small**,** we had to sell some of our furniture.*

A. Combine the sentences with the conjunction in parentheses. Pay attention to punctuation.

1. Do you only buy things you really need? Do you buy things that catch your eye? (or)

   _____

2. I've decided to stop buying luxury goods. It's better for the environment. (since)

   _____

3. My house has a lot of things in it. It's still neat and attractive. (although)

   _____

4. I always think about whether I really need something. I buy it. (before)

   _____

5. People think items made from recycled materials are better for the environment. They often buy more of them. (so)

   _____

6. You can return an unnecessary item to the store. You kept the receipt. (provided that)

   _____

B. Complete the sentences. Then share your sentences with a partner.

1. Having a lot of personal objects in my home is / isn't important to me because

   _____.

2. Shopping relaxes / doesn't relax me, and _____

   _____.

(continued)

3. Used items are cheaper than new ones, so _____

_____.

4. Sometimes I feel bad about making a purchase after _____

_____.

5. Before I learned about how plastic packaging was made, _____

_____.

6. Items on sale in a store aren't always very cheap, yet _____

_____.

EXERCISE 5

A. *On a separate piece of paper, write two or three sentences to answer each question below. Use a different conjunction in each sentence. Use the chart to help you. You may use other words and phrases.*

Coordinating Conjunctions	Time Order	Cause	Contrast	Condition / Reason
for, and, nor, but, or, yet, so	after, as soon as, before, since, when, until	as, because, since	although, even though, whereas, while	provided that, so that

1. Do you think people can be addicted to shopping?

2. Do you buy more or fewer things than most of your friends?

3. Have you ever bought something because of an ad you saw online or on TV?

4. Do you think most advertisements are truthful?

5. Do you follow a monthly budget?

6. Are you more likely to buy an item if it's on sale?

B. *Compare your work with another student.*

EXERCISE 6

A. *Rewrite these paragraphs on a separate piece of paper. Combine sentences using coordinating and subordinating conjunctions. You may add, remove, or change words, but keep the main ideas. Remember to use the correct punctuation.*

I don't agree that giving up shopping for a year is a good idea. It sounds clever. It isn't very practical. Not everything that people buy is a luxury. I think shopping wisely is a better idea. You have to spend some of your money. You will make purchases that will last for a long time.

Most people throw things away when they are still good. They get tired of their things. They want to buy the latest fashions. They want to own the latest gadgets. They don't really need all of those new toys. They see a lot of advertisements. The advertisements make them believe they need those products. People should use what they have until the products wear out or break. That's less wasteful.

B. *Work in a group. Take turns reading your paragraphs aloud. How are they different?*

EXERCISE 7

A. *Work with another student. Exchange the object descriptions you wrote for the Warm Up on page 48. Discuss these questions:*

- Does the writing include a mix of short and longer sentences?

- Can your partner improve any of the sentences by adding more information or combining them?

- What adjectives, adverbs, prepositional phrases, or conjunctions can you suggest adding?

B. *Rewrite your paragraph following your partner's suggestions.*

WRITING TASK

Write a short composition about what and how much you buy.

Choose one of these topics and write a short composition of one to three paragraphs. Use prepositional phrases and conjunctions to expand and combine sentences.

- Is clutter (having too many things) a problem in your home or in the home of someone you know? Why do you think your home is cluttered? What can you do about it?

- Do you prefer to buy a lot of inexpensive things, or just a few expensive things? Why?

- How many times do you purchase something on an average day? What kinds of things do you buy?

- Would you buy a used product instead of a new one? Why or why not? What are some things that people should buy used? What are some things they should only buy new?

- How long could you go without buying anything new (not counting food)? What would be hardest for you to give up?

Check Your Writing

A. *Use this form to check your own composition, or exchange compositions with another student and check each other's writing.*

Composition Checklist

1. How many paragraphs does the composition have? _____

2. Does each paragraph follow the guidelines for good paragraphs? _____
   (See pages 32–33.)

3. What is the main idea of the composition? _____

4. Underline the prepositional phrases. How many are there? _____

5. Circle the coordinating conjunctions. How many are there? _____

6. Circle the subordinating conjunctions. How many are there? _____

7. What is your favorite short sentence from the composition? Copy it here:

   _____

8. What is your favorite longer sentence? Copy it here: _____

   _____

   _____

9. Are there any sentences that can be expanded or combined with prepositional phrases or conjunctions? Write your suggested changes here:

   _____

   _____

   _____

   _____

   _____

B. *Make changes to improve your composition. Remember to check your writing for grammar, spelling, and punctuation errors.*

UNIT 3

Relating Ideas

As you learn to expand sentences, and combine sentences into paragraphs and paragraphs into compositions and essays, it's important to use connecting words and punctuation to help the reader clearly see the connections between ideas.

This unit reviews and practices useful ways to show relationships between ideas in writing.

Warm Up

A. *Work in a group. Look at the pictures. Discuss these questions:*

- What are some talents or abilities you have?
- Do you think certain people are born with natural talents?
- Describe someone you know who has an interesting talent or ability.

B. *Do a five-minute freewrite about one of the ideas or people you talked about in Exercise A.*

RELATIVE PRONOUNS AND ADVERBS

Relative clauses can be used to add more information to a sentence, as well as to connect and relate ideas. Relative clauses begin with a **relative pronoun** (such as *that*, *which*, *who*, or *whom*) or a **relative adverb** (such as *where* or *when*).

Relative Pronouns	Relative Adverbs
that	where
which	when
who / whom	

These pronouns and adverbs can be used to connect two sentences. They connect to the main sentence and give more information about it. They may function as either the subject or the object of the clause.

Examples:

James is a boy. James won the talent competition.
*James is the boy **who** won the talent competition.*

There's a dance school. I attended the dance school.
*There's the dance school **that** I attended.*

There's the dance school. I had my first lessons there.
*There's the dance school **where** I had my first lessons.*

The competition was extremely difficult. It included applicants from all over the country.
*The competition, **which** included applicants from all over the country, was extremely difficult.*

Note: In conversation and informal writing, many fluent English speakers use *who* for both subjects and objects. In formal writing, however, *whom* is used for objects.

Example:

Informal: *Dr. Carter is the expert **who** I consulted.*
Formal: *Dr. Carter is the expert **whom** I consulted.*

EXERCISE 1

Complete the sentences with who, whom, that, which, when, *or* where. *Use* whom *for objects.*

1. In the town _____ I grew up, there weren't many opportunities to study art.

2. Maria Jimenez, _____ was my friend in elementary school, taught herself to paint by looking at library books.

3. Maria was one of those people _____ had a natural talent and also a lot of ambition.

4. She was "discovered" by an art gallery owner _____ she was in high school.

5. That gallery owner, _____ I really respect, helped Maria pay to attend art school after she graduated.

6. These days, she creates paintings and sculptures, _____ she sells for thousands of dollars.

7. She donated some of her paintings to the library _____ she checked out her first art books.

8. Maria's story shows that it's important to have someone _____ believes in you.

EXERCISE 2

Combine the two sentences by making one a relative clause. Write new sentences on a separate piece of paper. Add relative pronouns and adverbs as necessary. Follow the example.

Example:

Mr. Smith is a teacher. Mr. Smith has taught me a lot.

Mr. Smith is a teacher who has taught me a lot.

1. Running is a sport. You can do that sport just about anywhere.
2. I had a great running coach, Jeff Hess. I had him in high school.
3. Mr. Hess was a coach. He taught me both physical and mental skills.
4. The track is a place. I can work on myself as a person there.
5. I go running at times. At those times I feel confused or stressed.
6. I ran in competitive races. I was younger at that time.
7. Today, running is something I do. I run just for enjoyment.
8. These days, I like to run with other people. I like people who are not competitive.

EXERCISE 3

Complete the sentences with a relative pronoun and your own ideas. Share your sentences with another student.

1. A good teacher is someone _____.

2. Learning something new is an experience _____.

3. Playing a musical instrument is a skill _____.

4. I don't know anyone _____.

(continued)

5. _____ is a friend _____ .
　　　your friend's name

6. Do you know of a Web site _____ ?

7. Can you recommend a book _____ ?

8. Being able to _____ is a talent _____ .
　　　　　　　　one of your talents

9. My home is a place _____ .

10. I can't remember a time _____ .

DEPENDENT AND INDEPENDENT RELATIVE CLAUSES

Dependent relative clauses (also called _restrictive relative clauses_) must be joined to the main sentence. If you remove these clauses from the sentence, the main sentence is incorrect.

> **_Example:_**
>
> _James is the boy **who** won the talent competition._
>
> (_James is the boy_ is not a complete, correct sentence. Therefore, the clause is dependent.)

There is no comma before or after a dependent relative clause.

Independent relative clauses (also called _non-restrictive relative clauses_) can be removed from the original sentence, leaving a grammatically acceptable sentence.

> **_Example:_**
>
> _The competition, **which** included applicants from all over the country, was extremely difficult._
>
> (_The competition was extremely difficult._ is a complete, correct sentence, so the clause is independent.)

Independent relative clauses are preceded and followed by a comma (or just preceded by one if they finish the sentence).

Notes:

- Do not use a comma before or after a dependent relative clause.
  Examples:
  > Correct: _This is the award that I won in the singing competition._
  > Incorrect: _This is the award, that I won in the singing competition._

- Use a comma before an independent relative clause if it ends the sentence.
  Example:
  > _This is the award from the singing competition, which I won._

- Use a comma both before and after an independent relative clause in the middle of a sentence.
  Example:
  > _The award, which I won in a singing competition, was a silver microphone._

- In conversation and informal English, _which_ and _that_ are used in both dependent and independent clauses. In formal written American English, _that_ is used for dependent clauses, and _which_ is used for independent clauses.

Read the paragraph. Underline the relative clauses. Decide whether they are dependent or independent. Then add commas where necessary. (Do not remove any commas.)

I never thought I had any particular talent when I was growing up. In fact, I was convinced that I wasn't as clever as my older brother who was good at sports or my younger sister who excelled in English. I didn't change my mind until I started high school where I met Ms. Hocken. She was the teacher for both physics and chemistry which were the hardest classes I have ever taken. However, she was an excellent teacher. She was encouraging and patient, and she gave us lots of practical examples that helped us understand why the theories were important and useful. The first time I went to see her in her office when I had failed a test she told me she thought I was good at science. I was so surprised. No teacher had told me before that I was good at something. She let me repeat the test which I passed the second time, and after that, I worked extra hard in her classes. I think I actually became good at science because she told me that I was good at science. You could say that she created my talent. I had many good teachers in high school, but of all of them, Ms. Hocken is the one whom I admire the most.

CONNECTING SENTENCES WITH TRANSITIONS

In Unit 2, you practiced ways to connect ideas in one sentence. **Transitions** are words and phrases that connect one sentence or idea to the next. The following chart lists common transitions and their purposes.

Adding Information	Comparing	Contrasting	Giving Examples	Explaining
Furthermore, . . . In addition, . . . Moreover, . . .	In the same way, . . . Likewise, . . . Similarly, . . .	However, . . . On the other hand, . . .	For example, . . . For instance, . . .	In other words, . . . That is to say, . . . Therefore, To put it another way, . . .

You have probably seen these transitions and used them to help you understand reading texts. Using them in your writing will help readers follow your ideas.

Often, transitions come at the beginning of a sentence in order to make a connection to the sentence just before. A comma comes after the transition:

Examples:

> Musical talent runs in my family. **For instance,** *my older sisters both play the violin.*
>
> *I love to play the cello.* **However,** *I hate to practice for my lessons.*

You can also use a semicolon to join the two sentences:

Examples:

> Musical talent runs in my family**; for instance,** *my older sisters both play the violin.*
>
> *I love to play the cello;* **however,** *I hate to practice for my lessons.*

Some transitions can also come in the middle of a sentence, typically between the subject and the verb. The expression is preceded and followed by a comma:

Examples:

> Musical talent runs in my family. My older sisters, **for instance,** both play the violin.
>
> *I love to play the cello. Practicing for my lessons,* **however,** *I don't enjoy as much.*

EXERCISE 5

A. **Complete the paragraph with transitions from the chart on page 61. More than one answer is possible.**

When I was a child, I took piano lessons. At first, I enjoyed them a lot. I liked being able to make beautiful music, and learning new songs didn't seem difficult to me. (**1.**) _____ , I felt good about it because I got a lot of positive attention from my friends and family. (**2.**) _____ , they would say, "Great job!" or "You play so well."

Later, (**3.**) _____ , playing the piano became more stressful. My piano teacher asked me to take part in recitals and concerts, and I felt very nervous on stage. I told my parents I wanted to stop taking lessons. They argued with me for a while, saying that I had a talent. But I said I didn't feel that having a talent should mean that I had to continue something I didn't enjoy. (**4.**) _____ , I quit. For a while, I was much happier, and I think it was the right choice.

(**5.**) _____ , sometimes I wish my parents had forced me to stick with it; I'd be an amazing musician today.

B. *Compare paragraphs with another student.*

Further Practice

Journal or Blog Topics *(See Part 1, Units 1 and 2.)*

- Write a paragraph about a teacher who helped you develop a skill or talent. What did this teacher do that helped you learn the skill?

- Write a paragraph about your experience trying to learn something new. Was it easy, challenging, frustrating? Why? Did you continue, or did you give up?

EXERCISE 6

A. *Connect the ideas. Match the sentences on the left with sentences on the right. More than one answer is possible.*

_____ **1.** I wanted to be a violinist.

_____ **2.** I took lessons for three years.

_____ **3.** You don't have to pay for lessons to learn something.

_____ **4.** I don't believe in "talent."

_____ **5.** Talent is important.

_____ **6.** Some children start music lessons when they are two or three years old.

_____ **7.** Some high school students have sports or music practice every day after school.

_____ **8.** It's important for young people to practice hard and develop their skills.

a. I never enjoyed them.

b. You become good at something through lots of hard work.

c. They spend all weekend taking lessons.

d. Having friends and enjoying life is important, too

e. I hated practicing.

f. It doesn't matter how hard you practice if you don't have a natural ability.

g. I learned salsa dance by watching videos online.

h. I think that's really too early.

B. *Choose a transition to connect each pair of sentences from Exercise A. Write your new sentences on a separate sheet of paper. Then compare them with another student. (More than one answer is possible.)*

EXERCISE 7

Check your freewrite from the Warm Up. Change at least two sentences to include transitions.

AVOIDING PROBLEMS

Joining sentences and clauses together to make longer, more complex sentences can make your writing more sophisticated and interesting. However, these longer sentences can be difficult to punctuate correctly. In this section, you will examine some common punctuation errors and ways to fix them.

Run-On Sentences

A run-on sentence consists of two independent clauses (a clause that contains a subject and a verb) that have not been correctly connected.

> **Example:**
>
> **Incorrect:** *I would rather be good at many things than just one thing I like sports as well as music and painting.*

There are several ways to fix a run-on sentence:

1. Divide it into two sentences:

   > **Example:**
   >
   > *I would rather be good at many things than just one thing. I like sports as well as music and painting.*

2. Add a conjunction (See Part 2, Unit 2.):

   > **Examples:**
   >
   > *I would rather be good at many things than just one thing **because** I like sports as well as music and painting.*
   >
   > ***Because** I like sports as well as music and painting, I would rather be good at many things than just one thing.*

3. Add a transition and the appropriate punctuation:

   > **Example:**
   >
   > *I would rather be good at many things than just one thing; **for example,** I like sports as well as music and painting.*

A. *Check (✓) the correct sentences. Mark the run-on sentences with an X.*

_____ **1.** Some people think that playing is a waste of children's time they think that children should spend more time learning.

_____ **2.** Playing is important for children they are actually learning something valuable.

_____ **3.** Playing is actually a way for children to learn and practice the skills they need to survive in their environment.

_____ **4.** Some types of play help children develop important physical skills, such as running, climbing, and jumping.

_____ **5.** Other types of play teach mental skills children learn to think critically and make decisions.

_____ **6.** Social interaction with another child or with a group of children is important, too.

_____ **7.** Children can learn how to negotiate and compromise they will need these skills as adults.

_____ **8.** Even animals play lion and tiger cubs play in order to practice hunting.

_____ **9.** Parents and teachers need to understand the importance of play.

_____ **10.** They will tell their children and students, "Go play" in addition to "Get to work."

B. *Write a paragraph using the information from Exercise A. Fix any run-on sentences and join at least two sentences with a transition.*

C. *Compare paragraphs with another student. How are they similar? How are they different?*

Comma Splices

Comma splices occur when two independent clauses are incorrectly connected with a comma.

The comma might be incorrectly used in place of a period:

Example:

Incorrect: *Author Malcolm Gladwell did some interesting research on professional Canadian hockey players, he noticed they had something unusual in common.*

A comma splice may occur before a subordinating conjunction or a transition:

Example:

Incorrect: *He found that most of them were born in January, February, or March, then he decided to find out why.*

You can fix comma splices is several ways.

1. Make two sentences:

   Example:

   Author Malcolm Gladwell did some interesting research on professional Canadian hockey players. He noticed they had something unusual in common.

2. Use a coordinating conjunction after the comma:

   Examples:

   *He found that most of them were born in January, February, or March, **so** he decided to find out why.*

   *He found that most of them were born in January, February, or March, **and then** he decided to find out why.*

3. Use a semicolon + transition + comma:

   Example:

   *He found that most of them were born in January, February, or March**; therefore,** he decided to find out why.*

4. Rearrange the clauses:

   Example:

   He decided to find out why most of them were born in January, February, or March.

arrived. In fact, I had to wait for four days before my bag came—and my vacation was only five days long! And no one apologized to me. I have flown with that airline for many years, but now I am thinking about trying a different one.

EXERCISE 3

Work with a partner or group. Look at the word map you made in the Warm Up about a vacation. Choose one story from that vacation and tell it to your group. Add more information to your word map if you can.

ADVERBS WITH THE PRESENT PERFECT AND THE SIMPLE PAST

The present perfect can be a challenging verb tense because it is used in several different ways. In addition, it is not used in the same way or does not exist in some other languages.

However, it is very common in English, so it's important to continue to practice using the present perfect and the simple past correctly.

There are several adverbs that are commonly used with the present perfect:

ever   never   yet   already   for   since

Examples:

For questions about experiences

> *Have you **ever** been to Canada?*

For experiences and actions not done

> *I've **never** flown in a helicopter.*

For questions and negative statements about whether an action is done

> *Have you bought any postcards **yet**? / I haven't bought any postcards **yet**.*

For experiences that happened earlier than expected

> *My brother has **already** been to every continent.*

To express action done for a duration of time

> *I've been planning this vacation **for** several months.*

To express action that began at a specific point in time

> *I've been planning this vacation **since** January.*

When *for* and *since* are not used, adverbs of time such as *today, last week, the day before yesterday, the year before last, in 2009, ago,* and so on usually signal the simple past (for one event already completed).

Examples:

> *I booked my hotel last month.*
> *I took a tour of the state capitol in 2010.*
> *I went on a class trip to Kyoto three years ago.*

Complete the paragraph with adverbs from the box. You can use the same adverb more than once.

ago	already	before	ever	for	last	never	since	yet

My Bucket List

Have you (**1.**) _____ heard the term "bucket list"? It's a slang term for a list of things that you want to do or see in your lifetime. I made such a list in high school, just for fun, and then I forgot about it. Well, I found that list the other day, and it was interesting to see which of the things I've (**2.**) _____ done and which I haven't done (**3.**) _____. I hadn't thought about that list (**4.**) _____ high school, but obviously, I was dreaming a lot about travel. I did get a chance to travel three years (**5.**) _____ when I took a trip across Canada. So I've (**6.**) _____ ridden a train, and I've gone camping. I've also climbed a mountain, and I've ridden a horse—in fact, I rode one for the first time the summer (**7.**) _____ last. Now, I haven't done everything on my list (**8.**) _____. I've (**9.**) _____ taken a trip in a boat or a ship. I almost had a chance last summer, but I did something else instead. Still, if I've had it on a list (**10.**) _____ more than seven years, I'm sure I will do it someday!

A. **On a separate piece of paper, write questions to ask a partner about his or her travel and vacation experiences. Write at least six questions using the present perfect. Write follow up questions using the simple past or simple present.**
Examples:

Have you ever traveled abroad?
> (if yes) *Where did you go?*
> (if no) *Do you want to go abroad?*

Have you ever written a bucket list?
> (if yes) *What did you include on it?*

B. *Work with another student. Take turns asking and answering your questions. Take notes on your partner's answers.*

C. *Use your notes to write a paragraph about the experiences your partner has and hasn't had. Check your paragraph for correct verb tenses.*

ACTIVE VOICE AND PASSIVE VOICE

Sentences in English with an action verb—a verb such as *play*, *run*, or *create*—can be in either the **active** or the **passive** voice.

Active sentences are the most common. In an active sentence, the <u>subject</u> does the action, and the action happens to the <u>object</u>.

> **Examples:**
>
> <u>My travel agent</u> bought <u>the train tickets</u>.
>
> <u>Christopher Wren</u> designed <u>St. Paul's Cathedral</u>.

In a passive sentence, the object moves in front of the verb to become the subject—yet it still receives the action. The former subject moves to the end of the sentence, or is omitted altogether:

> <u>The train tickets</u> were bought a few weeks ago (by my travel agent).
>
> <u>St. Paul's Cathedral</u> was built in the 17th century.

The passive voice is common in the following situations:

1. When the subject of the sentence is not known, or is not important

> **Example:**
>
> St. Paul's Cathedral was built in the 17th century.
>
> **NOT**
>
> They / People / Workers built St. Paul's Cathedral in the 17th century.

2. To describe a process or explain how something was done

> **Example:**
>
> The stones were placed one by one.

3. To emphasize the name of a location, building, monument, company, etc.

> **Examples:**
>
> The city of Paris was founded around 250 BCE.
>
> The ruins were discovered by a British archaeologist.

Common verbs used in the passive include the following examples:

was built in	*was constructed in / by*	*is visited by*	*are enjoyed by*
was founded by	*were discovered in*	*can be seen by*	*can be found in*

> **Note:** Some word processing software marks every usage of the passive, and this can lead some writers to worry that the passive is "wrong." It isn't. Although it isn't used as much as the active, sometimes the passive is the best choice.

A. *Read the pairs of sentences. Check (✓) whether you prefer the active or the passive version. Note that all sentences are grammatically correct. Select the sentence you think sounds better.*

1. ☐ **a.** The main part of Stonehenge is made up of a circle of large standing stones.

   ☐ **b.** Large standing stones make up the main part of Stonehenge.

2. ☐ **a.** Stonehenge was probably created around 2500 BCE.

   ☐ **b.** Whoever created Stonehenge probably did so around 2500 BCE.

3. ☐ **a.** Stonehenge is believed by some archaeologists to be an ancient burial ground.

   ☐ **b.** Some archaeologists believe that Stonehenge was an ancient burial ground.

4. ☐ **a.** Others maintain that Stonehenge was used mainly for religious purposes.

   ☐ **b.** Others maintain that people used Stonehenge mainly for religious purposes.

5. ☐ **a.** Stonehenge has been restored several times in the last few hundred years.

   ☐ **b.** Different groups of people have restored Stonehenge several times in the last few hundred years.

6. ☐ **a.** Some tools, weapons, and even a container of drink were uncovered during some of the restorations.

   ☐ **b.** Archaeologists uncovered tools, weapons, and even a container of drink during some of the restorations.

7. ☐ **a.** When Stonehenge was first opened to the public, visitors were allowed to touch the stones and even climb on them.

   ☐ **b.** When the organization taking care of Stonehenge at the time first opened the site to the public, it allowed visitors to touch the stones and even climb on them.

8. ☐ **a.** Stonehenge is visited by around 800,000 people each year.

   ☐ **b.** Around 800,000 people visit Stonehenge each year.

B. *Compare your choices with a partner. Discuss any different opinions. You might not agree on which one sounds better.*

Further Practice

Research and Write

- Choose a building, monument, or tourist site that interests you. Use a location connected to the word map you did for the Warm Up, or choose a different one.
- Find out information about the site (dates and other interesting facts). Use the Internet, books, or other resources you can find.
- On a separate piece of paper, write five sentences to describe the monument. Use the passive voice.
- Share your sentences with another student.

Journal or Blog Topic *(See Part 1, Units 1 and 2.)*

- Imagine your class has won a million dollars to take a dream vacation.
- Write your ideas for the class trip. Then have a class discussion to decide where the class should go.

WRITING TASK

Write a short composition about a vacation.

A. *Look at your word map from the Warm Up. Choose an aspect of that vacation to write about. For example, you could describe the entire vacation, just one story from it, or describe a monument or site you visited.*

B. *On a separate piece of paper, write a short composition (one to three paragraphs) about the vacation.*

Check Your Writing

A. *Use this form to check your own composition, or exchange compositions with another student and check each other's writing.*

Composition Checklist

1. What is the main idea of the composition? _____

2. How is the composition organized? As a story? As a group of events? As a description?
_____

3. Circle all of the verbs. Are the verb tenses used correctly? _____
_____

4. Underline any passive sentences. Are they used correctly? _____
_____

5. What is your favorite sentence from the composition? Copy it here: _____
_____
_____

6. Are there any sentences that you didn't understand? If so, write a question mark (?) in front of them on the composition.

7. What ideas or suggestions do you have to improve the composition? Write your suggested changes here:
_____
_____
_____
_____
_____

B. *Make changes to improve your composition. Remember to check your writing for grammar, spelling, and punctuation errors.*

Figurative Language

Figurative language is often associated with descriptive, creative writing, but it is present in all types of writing. Examples of types of figurative language include simile, metaphor, extended metaphor, and personalization. These techniques help make a piece of writing more interesting, more powerful, and more expressive.

In this unit, you will discuss literal and figurative language; learn the characteristics of simile, metaphor, extended metaphor, and personification; and practice incorporating these techniques into your writing.

Warm Up

A. *Work in a group. Take turns describing the pictures.*

B. *Choose one picture and do a five-minute freewrite, describing the scene.*

LITERAL AND FIGURATIVE LANGUAGE

Words that are used in a **literal** sense have the same meaning as what you'd find in the dictionary.

Example:

We bought a new table for our apartment.

Here, *table* means "a piece of furniture." Literal language is often short, direct, and clear. Textbooks use a lot of literal language, and so do short informational letters and emails.

Words that are used in a **figurative** sense draw a comparison between one object or idea and another, either directly or indirectly.

Example:

The top of the cliff was as flat as a table.

Here, the top of the cliff is being compared to something else. The cliff is not a piece of furniture, but in a way, it resembles one.

(continued)

Example:

The setting sun colored the peaks and tables of the mountains red and gold.

Here, the cliff top is again compared to a table, though the comparison is more indirect. In addition, the sun is being compared to a painter.

Writers use figurative language to make their writing more interesting and varied. Figurative language can also give your writing more emotional impact. In addition, using these kinds of descriptive images helps your readers picture in their minds the scenes you are describing.

EXERCISE 1

A. **Work with another student. Discuss each situation. Would you use mostly literal language, mostly figurative language, or a mix of both? (Note that there are no wrong answers.)**

1. An essay for a university class

2. An email to a close friend

3. A poem about your hometown

4. A letter to the newspaper about a local issue

5. An article for a travel magazine about a city

6. A letter to a company complaining about a product

7. A blog entry about your weekend

8. A personal journal entry

B. **Join another pair. Discuss your ideas. Explain your opinions.**

EXERCISE 2

Work with a partner or group. Look at the freewriting you did for the Warm Up. Did you use more literal language or more figurative language?

A. *Read the sentences. Write* **L** *if the sentence uses only literal language. Write* **F** *if it uses figurative language.*

_____ **1.** Alejandro's eyes sparkled like stars.

_____ **2.** My sister's nose is long and straight.

_____ **3.** She carefully brushed her river of hair.

_____ **4.** The inspector towered over the child.

_____ **5.** The soft wind whispered in my ear.

_____ **6.** When she was young, my mother was a talented dancer.

_____ **7.** The curtains danced in the sunlight.

_____ **8.** My gym teacher is as strong as an ox.

_____ **9.** Amina is slender, but she's much stronger than she looks.

_____ **10.** Who is that man with the salt-and-pepper hair?

_____ **11.** She has an enchanting voice; I could listen all day to the music of her speech.

_____ **12.** The snow covered the landscape like a blanket.

_____ **13.** The forest vines grabbed at my ankles.

_____ **14.** My brother is several centimeters taller than my father.

_____ **15.** The rushing water laughed over the rocks as happily as a child.

B. *Work with another student. Look at the figurative sentences from Exercise A. What things are being compared? Are the figurative words nouns, adjectives, adverbs, or verbs?*

C. *Add any useful vocabulary or phrases from Exercise A to your vocabulary notebook. (See Part 2, Unit 1.)*

SIMILES

A **simile** is a figurative comparison that uses *like* or *as*:

like the wind	*as gentle as a kitten*
like a train	*as fast as lightning*
like the falling rain	*as smooth as silk*

Some similes are common phrases and are widely known in English. People are used to hearing these familiar comparisons, and it is useful to be familiar with common ones because you will encounter them in everyday speech as well as in writing.

A. *Match the two halves of the expressions to form commonly known expressions.*

_____ **1.** as light as	**a.** a bird
_____ **2.** as tough as	**b.** gold
_____ **3.** as sharp as	**c.** nails
_____ **4.** as dumb as	**d.** a fish
_____ **5.** eat like	**e.** a tack
_____ **6.** run like	**f.** a feather
_____ **7.** as good as	**g.** sugar
_____ **8.** as stubborn as	**h.** a mule
_____ **9.** swim like	**i.** a box of rocks
_____ **10.** as straight as	**j.** a mouse
_____ **11.** as sweet as	**k.** the wind
_____ **12.** as quiet as	**l.** an arrow

B. *Work with another student. Answer these questions about the expressions in Exercise A.*

- What does each one mean? Is it a compliment, an insult, or neither?
- Which ones have you heard before?
- Does a similar expression exist in your language?

C. *Add any useful vocabulary or phrases from Exercise A to your vocabulary notebook.*

Note: Some people consider common similes to be clichés—expressions that are repeated too often and are not fresh and interesting anymore. For this reason, you might prefer to create your own new similes when you write instead of trying to memorize ones already used in English.

EXERCISE 5

Work with another student. Create five new similes using phrases from Exercise 4A. You can change the first or the second half of the expression. Then join another pair and share your similes.

A. *Choose one of these topics. Brainstorm some similes to describe it. Then write a descriptive paragraph that includes some of your similes.*

- a friend or relative
- a person you dislike
- a favorite place
- a game or sport you enjoy
- an activity you hate

B. *Work in a group. Take turns reading your paragraphs aloud. Choose a favorite simile from each paragraph and share them with the class.*

METAPHOR, PERSONIFICATION, AND EXTENDED METAPHOR

A **metaphor** is a comparison that does <u>not</u> use *like* or *as*. If you describe clouds as *soft cotton puffs in the sky*, or a person's laughter with *he exploded in laughter*, you are using metaphor.

Personification is a special kind of metaphor in which an animal or object is described as though it is a person: *the icy fingers of the wind, the flowers danced in the breeze.*

An **extended metaphor**, sometimes called an analogy, is a comparison made in a longer text—several sentences, a paragraph, or even an entire essay. Metaphors are common in both poetry and prose.

A. *Read the two passages. Look up any words you don't know in a dictionary. Underline the metaphors.*

Passage 1

My Journey with Books

Good books are rocket ships to a new world. When I open a book and begin my journey, everything else just slips away. I forget about school, work, even the couch I'm sitting on.

Every Sunday, rain or shine, I go to the library by my house. The books on the shelves are like miniature rainbows—so pretty I could just stare at them all day. But I can't take them all home, so I pick my favorites, stacking them until I have a mountain of books in my arms.

The librarian is my tour guide, pointing out the best books, secret hidden treasures that I missed on my travels through the aisles. Sometimes she even keeps special books behind the counter for me, little gifts of paper and words that have my name written on them. Her eyes light up when she tells me about them.

"Do you have your passport to other worlds?" she asks me when it's time to check out. "I have it right here," I say, and I hand her the little plastic card that grants me access to a whole new world.

When I'm ready to go, she gives me a sunny smile, knowing that I will enjoy those books as much as she did. Our lives are woven together into a fabric made of the stories we read. As soon as I get all my treasures home, I become the world's biggest bookworm, devouring the stories as quickly as I can. Books are the best vacations I've ever taken. Outside of the library, that is.

Passage 2

<u>September 20, 2011</u>

It's been three weeks since I moved here. I've finally unpacked and put everything away. I've settled in. I'm home.

The view from my window stretches far to the east. In the distance, a slope-shouldered mountain range catches the sea-cloud and wears it like a cloak. Often in the mornings, thick mist sits in the valley, hiding the forest that reaches almost to the garden.

I walk in the woods most days, alongside the sulky brown river that winds through the trees. Old oaks trail their roots in the water as if testing the temperature before they decide whether to swim, and green reeds wave at the river, jostling to point it in the right direction as it rushes to the waiting lake.

B. *Work in a group. Discuss these questions:*

- What comparison does each metaphor in Passages 1 and 2 make?

- Do you think the metaphors are effective? Were there any that were hard to understand? Did the metaphors make it easier or more difficult for you to imagine the people, places, situations, and feelings?

- Which metaphors were examples of personification?

- Were any similes used? If so, where?

C. *Add any useful vocabulary or phrases from the passages to your vocabulary notebook.*

A. *Write a paragraph to describe each photo. Use similes, personification, and metaphors.*

B. *Exchange paragraphs with another student. Can you tell which picture is being described in each one? How are your descriptions the same? How are they different?*

C. *Check the freewriting you did for the Warm Up again. Add some similes, metaphors, and personification.*

Note: Like some similes, some metaphors are used so often in English that they have become too common, and can make a piece of writing sound predictable or even boring. For this reason, it's best to use your own original comparisons when possible.

A. *Read this famous poem by the American poet Robert Frost (1874–1963). The entire poem is an extended metaphor.*

The Road Not Taken

Two roads diverged in a yellow wood,
And sorry I could not travel both
And be one traveler, long I stood
And looked down one as far as I could
To where it bent in the undergrowth;

Then took the other, as just as fair,
And having perhaps the better claim,
Because it was grassy and wanted wear;
Though as for that the passing there
Had worn them really about the same,

And both that morning equally lay
In leaves no step had trodden black.
Oh, I kept the first for another day!
Yet knowing how way leads on to way,
I doubted if I should ever come back.

I shall be telling this with a sigh
Somewhere ages and ages hence:
Two roads diverged in a wood, and I—
I took the one less traveled by,
And that has made all the difference.

B. *Work in a group. Discuss the metaphor in the poem. What does the "road" represent? What does each stanza (group of lines) in the poem mean, both literally and figuratively?*

Further Practice

Journal or Blog Topic *(See Part 1, Units 1 and 2.)*

• Find a poem or a passage (from a short story, novel, or other piece of fiction writing) in English that includes examples of similes or metaphor. Write your favorite examples and explain why you like them.

WRITING TASK

Write a short descriptive composition using figurative language.

A. **Choose one of these topics. Write a short composition (two to three paragraphs) to describe it. Use an extended metaphor and include other examples of figurative language (similes, metaphor, personification).**

- Love
- Fear
- Work
- Growing old
- Friendship
- Travel
- Music
- Reading
- Childhood
- School / Studying / Learning
- Your idea _____

Example:

Life is like a journey. You travel different paths, some that other people have traveled before you . . .

B. **Work in a group. Take turns reading your compositions aloud. For each group member's description, write down one or two examples of simile, metaphor, or personification that you liked. Then share them with the class.**

Check Your Writing

A. **Use this form to check your own composition, or exchange compositions with another student and check each other's writing.**

> ### Composition Checklist
>
> 1. Underline the examples of similes in the composition. How many are there? _____
>
> 2. Circle the examples of metaphors. How many are there? _____
>
> 3. Are there any examples of personification? Copy them here: _____
> _____
>
> 4. What is your favorite example of figurative language from the composition? Copy it here:
> _____
>
> 5. Do you have any ideas or suggestions for places to add figurative language in the composition? Write them here: _____
> _____
> _____

B. **Make changes to improve your composition. Remember to check your writing for grammar, spelling, and punctuation errors.**

Academic Writing

Introduction

In this part of *Writing Power 3* you will work on developing skills for academic writing—writing you do for high school or university classes. You will study and practice all of the elements you will need to write an academic essay.

As you will see, academic writing requires special skills. First you will learn and practice these skills individually, and then you will put them together to write academic papers and essays. Skills introduced in Part 3 include the following:

- Paragraphs and Patterns of Organization
- Summary Writing
- Working with Source Materials
- Prewriting Techniques
- Thesis Statements, Introductions, and Conclusions
- Organizing and Drafting
- Revising and Proofreading
- Timed Essays

UNIT 1

What Is Academic Writing?

Academic writing is writing you do for high school, college, or university. Your teacher may ask you to write a report about a book you have read, an essay responding to a topic or question, or a research paper about an issue you have studied. This type of writing usually requires you to analyze and explain a topic, form an opinion, and then support it.

Academic writing requires special skills and knowledge. For academic writing, you need to follow certain rules for format and language use that are different from other types of writing. For example, think about writing a text message to a friend. How is it different from writing an assignment for school? What do you do when you write a text message? What do you do when you write an essay?

In this unit you will learn and practice what makes academic writing different from other types of writing.

Warm Up

A. *Look at the list of activities. Do they relate to writing text messages or school assignments? Write T for text messages or S for school assignments. Write B for both, if the activity relates to both.*

____ Write about one topic

____ Gather information about a topic

____ Brainstorm ideas about your topic

____ Organize or outline your ideas

____ Include a topic sentence

____ Write about one main idea

____ Write two or more paragraphs

____ Follow a special format

____ Include an introduction, body paragraphs, and a conclusion

____ Use complete sentences

____ Use informal language

____ Use formal language

____ Write for your teacher

____ Write for your classmates

____ Write for your friends

____ Write about weekend plans, school events, or personal topics

____ Write about a problem

____ Check your writing for errors

____ Write about social issues, scientific studies, or political topics

B. *Compare answers with another student. Which skills from the list above do you feel you need to improve most?*

WRITING FOR AN AUDIENCE

Whenever and whatever you write, you are writing for a particular reader or audience. In writing you do outside of school, your audience may be a friend or family member, a future employer, or it may be you alone. When you write for academic purposes, your audience is your teacher, and sometimes your classmates.

In addition to the topic, the audience determines the language, tone, and style of a piece of writing.

EXERCISE 1

A. *Write the correct topic and audience from the box under each passage.*

Topic	Audience
a study meeting	a classmate
a development in medical science	the writer himself or herself
an event plan	students in a medical program
the definition of success	a family member
a journal entry	an English professor

New drug safety studies indicate that two widely used medicines, one for diabetes, the other for cholesterol, may lead to higher risks for heart attacks and strokes. The studies reopen concerns about approving medicines before all potential dangers have been ruled out. In this case, these medicines are supposed to lower risks for heart attacks and strokes. Instead, the medicines may be causing them.

1. Topic: _____ Audience: _____

What r u doing after school? Can u meet me in the library to work on project for psych class? lmk what time is ok for u. OK?

2. Topic: _____ Audience: _____

Who is the most successful person in the world—the president, the highest paid executive, a family member? Many people consider those with material wealth highly successful. Who does not sometimes imagine having millions of dollars? However, wealth cannot be the only factor when determining success and failure. Success is much broader and more complex than winning the lottery or inheriting family treasures. Success, according to many people, may be a goal you reach, being satisfied at work, or having positive relationships with family, friends, and coworkers.

3. Topic: _____ Audience: _____

Send me pix so i can put them on our site for the upcoming reunion on March 23. when i have the other stuff we talked about i will email you with the information you need. it was great seeing you at Aunt Karen's the other day. looking forward to working out more details for our get-together. it's going to be a great time.

4. Topic: _____ Audience: _____

Tuesday. It was the first day of classes. So many new things. I am really excited about my classes, except for the listening class. I am really going to have a lot of homework. It is also my weakest area. Why does everyone talk so fast everywhere—the teacher, people on television, my classmates? I met some new classmates today. They are from China, Brazil, and Italy. I really miss my family. I wonder what they are doing right now ...

5. Topic: _____ Audience: _____

B. *Compare answers with another student. Explain how you identified the audience.*

TONE AND REGISTER

Tone is an important quality of academic writing. The tone of a piece of writing is the mood created by the writer's choice of style. The tone can be friendly, funny, casual, serious, or intelligent. In order to successfully write for academic assignments, you need to know how to create the appropriate tone.

Register refers to the specific language (words, phrases, or expressions) you choose to express yourself. That is, we speak and write differently depending on the formality of the situation or our relationship to the person we are communicating with. Think about the way you speak to your friends, parents, boss, or teacher. How do you change the way you speak to each of them?

School is considered a formal setting. Depending on your class, you may use more informal (casual) language when you speak with your classmates and your teacher. However, no matter how informally you may speak to one another, when you write school assignments, you will need to use formal language.

As a language learner, learning the difference between formal and informal register may be a challenge. However, with time and practice, you can achieve your end goal—a well-written academic essay.

Guidelines for Using Formal Register

Using formal language means choosing the kind of vocabulary found in textbooks or formal documents.

- Avoid the use of slang (overly casual language) and incorrect spelling.

    Examples:

    ~~kids~~ → *children*   ~~See ya~~ → *Good-bye*

    ~~gonna~~ → *going to*   ~~wanna~~ → *want to*

- Avoid contractions such as *I'm* or *Where's*, or abbreviations such as *What r u doin?*

- Use a variety of sentence types and structures, including simple, compound, complex. (See Part 2, Unit 2 for more on sentence variety.)

- Avoid personal pronouns where possible. Instead, use impersonal expressions such as *There is/are*, *It is*, and passive verbs.

    Examples:

    ~~I interviewed 30 people for this report.~~ → *Thirty people were interviewed for this report.*

    ~~I have eaten many different kinds of chocolate.~~ → *There are many different kinds of chocolate.*

- Check your writing to make sure it is as free of errors as possible.

Circle the word or phrase that has a more formal register.

1. therefore / so
2. but / however
3. and / in addition
4. have to / hafta
5. I think / In my opinion
6. It is / It's
7. wrong / incorrect
8. lots of / many
9. guy / man
10. things / stuff
11. wonderful / awesome
12. also / furthermore
13. since / because
14. In other words, / I mean
15. you should / it is recommended
16. maybe / perhaps
17. frequently / all the time
18. wanna / want to

A. **Read the descriptions of formal and informal language.**

Formal	Informal
• Uses formal (textbook-like) vocabulary and phrases (*For example, Perhaps, However, . . . In addition, . . .*) • Includes longer, varied sentence types (simple, compound, complex) • Uses correct grammar, spelling, and punctuation • Uses a mix of active and passive verbs	• Starts sentences with coordinating conjunctions such as *and, so,* and *but* • Allows slang or casual expressions • Uses contractions and abbreviations • Uses informal punctuation (for example, overuse of exclamation points), and spelling (for example, *How r u?*)

B. **Read the sentences. Write F next to the ones with a formal register. Write I next to the ones with an informal register.**

_____ 1. Studies have shown that cheating is on the rise in sports, schools, and business.

_____ 2. Lately we've been hearing lots of stories in the news about athletes using performance-enhancing drugs.

_____ 3. Many student athletes are tempted to use performance-enhancing drugs, called steroids, because they think it is the only way they can win.

_____ 4. Student athletes are frequently unaware of the dangerous side effects of steroid use; for example, hair loss, nausea, and heart failure.

(continued)

5. But I think that these athletes are crazy to ruin their careers by using steroids.

6. Academic cheating may be increasing because students feel pressure to get good grades.

7. I wonder why there're so many students cheating on tests all the time!?!

8. More than 56 percent of MBA students are cheating, according to a study by the Center for Academic Integrity at Duke University.

9. I can't understand why anyone would wanna risk going to jail for stealing exam answers.

10. The need for business ethics classes increases with each arrest of a highly successful financier who cheats his or her loyal clients out of millions of dollars.

C. *On a separate piece of paper, rewrite the sentences you marked with an I. Make them appropriate for academic writing. Then compare your work with another student.*

SHORT ACADEMIC ESSAYS

Most short academic essays consist of about three to five paragraphs and are about 250–500 words long. Short essay topics usually do not require a lot of research. Your teacher may ask you to write a short essay on a personal topic or experience, or in response to a question or something you have read.

Essay Structure

As you have learned in this unit, it is important to consider audience and register when beginning a piece of academic writing.

In addition, all academic writing has certain features and follows the same general structure or form.

An academic essay . . .

- uses formal language.
- is about one topic.
- has a main idea or focus, called a thesis statement.
- begins with an introductory paragraph and ends with a concluding paragraph.
- has body paragraphs that give examples to support the writer's ideas.
- uses correct essay format.

Essay Formatting

Formatting refers to the way the text is arranged on the page. Academic essays usually follow a similar basic format.

Formatting considerations include . . .

- where to write your name, the date, and the name of your course.
- whether and where to include an essay title.
- the size of the margins.
- how much to indent each paragraph.
- how many spaces between the lines of text.

Your teacher will tell you if there are any additional formatting requirements.

EXERCISE 4

A. **Read the sample essay, "Volleyball Dreams." Check (✓) the structure and formatting features you find.**

☐ Body paragraphs   ☐ Double spacing   ☐ Introductory paragraph

☐ Concluding paragraph   ☐ Essay title   ☐ Single spacing

☐ Course title   ☐ Formal language   ☐ Writer's name

☐ Date   ☐ Indented paragraphs   ☐ Teacher's name

Caitlin Fedder
Writing 103
Professor Lier
June 7, 2012

Volleyball Dreams

Do you remember the classmate who never studied? The one who spent her free time with the troublemakers? That was me until one of my teachers, who was also the volleyball coach, insisted that I try out for the team. Playing volleyball changed my life. It gave me the opportunity to become physically fit, learn about being responsible, and develop useful life skills.

Physical fitness was never a priority for me. I had not enjoyed playing sports before, and after the first volleyball practice, I had had enough. The practice was strenuous and tedious, and I complained bitterly about it afterward. I told my

(continued)

teammates I was not planning to return the next day, but a group of them said, "Only babies quit," and challenged me to come to the next practice. I did come back the next day, and then my teammates encouraged me, saying that I had a strong serve. As a result, I kept coming back, and after a while, I could see and feel the difference the training was making. Physically, I began to feel stronger and less awkward. I also felt more confident. To my surprise, I began to look forward to our daily practice sessions.

Working with a team taught me to be responsible for my actions. First of all, my teammates depended on me. I knew that if I did not do my best, it would affect the whole team. I began to feel that if I missed a practice or a game, I might be the reason the team lost. In addition, when I tried my hardest, even if I failed, my teammates would say, "Good try" or "Don't worry about it." I quickly learned that when team members support each other, it can bring out the best in everyone.

Furthermore, playing a sport helped me build important life skills. Volleyball taught me the importance of having a goal. Suddenly, I wanted to win and be the best, which drove me to play with full concentration even when I felt frustrated. Lastly, I learned that rules are made for a reason. Following the rules makes the game fair and gives the players true satisfaction, whether they win or lose.

In conclusion, joining a volleyball team gave me a new sense of power and responsibility, and showed me the way to lead a healthy, productive life.

B. *Work with another student. Discuss these questions:*

- How many topics are there in the sample essay?
- In which paragraph does the writer introduce the topic of the essay?
- Which sentences in the introductory paragraph tell the writer's main point (thesis statement)?
- In what part of the essay does the writer give specific examples to support her main point?
- What information does the writer give in the concluding paragraph? Does she add any new information?
- What are some examples of formal register used in the essay?

WRITING TASK

Write a short essay about an experience that taught you something important.

A. *Choose one of these topics, or use your own idea.*

- Participating in a sport
- Joining a club or other group activity
- Visiting a new place
- Taking a class
- Trying something for the first time
- Meeting a new person
- Attending an event or a performance
- Making a mistake

B. *Use this form to help you organize your ideas.*

Topic: _____

Introduction:

What was the experience? _____

_____

What did you learn from it? _____

_____

_____

Body:

What are specific examples of what you learned from the experience?

_____

_____

_____

_____

_____

Conclusion:

What are the most important things you learned from the experience? How will you use what you learned in the future?

_____

_____

_____

C. *Write your essay on a separate piece of paper. Follow these instructions for structure and format:*

1. Write the following single-spaced in the upper left corner:

   your name   the course title

   the date   your teacher's name

2. Write a title for your writing. Center it above the introductory paragraph.

3. Write three to four paragraphs: Introduction (one paragraph); Body (one to two paragraphs); Conclusion (one paragraph).

4. Use double spacing for the main text.

5. Indent each paragraph.

Check Your Writing

A. *Use this form to check your writing, or exchange essays with another student and check each other's writing.*

Essay Checklist

The essay . . .

1. is the right length. ☐

2. follows the guidelines for formal register on page 94. ☐

3. focuses on one main topic. ☐

4. includes an introductory paragraph that explains the writer's main point. ☐

5. has a concluding paragraph. ☐

6. follows the correct format for name, date, course title, and teacher's name. ☐

7. follows the correct format for title, spacing, and indenting. ☐

8. Were there any sentences you didn't understand? If so, write a question mark (?) in front of them on the essay.

9. Underline one or two sentences in the essay that you particularly liked.

10. Do you have any questions? Write them here:

    _____

    _____

11. What changes do you suggest to improve the essay?

    _____

    _____

B. *Make changes to improve your essay. Remember to check your writing for grammar, spelling, and punctuation errors.*

UNIT 2

Paragraphs and Patterns of Organization

You have probably studied writing paragraphs before, and you may know many of the characteristics of a good paragraph. For example, all paragraphs are about one topic and have one main idea. Good paragraphs also include supporting sentences that all relate to and support the main idea. (See the Part 2 Introduction for more on writing good paragraphs.) In your previous writing classes, you may have also practiced writing paragraphs with a special purpose, like explaining how to do something or showing reasons why something happened.

In this unit, you will learn the basic elements of academic paragraph writing, and practice writing different types of paragraphs commonly assigned in academic courses.

Warm Up

*Work with another student. Read the characteristics of paragraphs. Write **A** next to the ones that describe all paragraphs. Write **S** next to the ones that describe some paragraphs. Mark an **X** next to the ones that are not characteristics of a paragraph.*

_____ is eight sentences long

_____ has a topic sentence at the beginning

_____ has one main idea

_____ gives examples

_____ presents facts

_____ ends with a concluding sentence

_____ solves a problem

_____ uses only complete sentences

_____ contrasts or compares two or more things

_____ is indented

_____ develops one topic

_____ contains supporting sentences or details

CHARACTERISTICS OF ACADEMIC PARAGRAPHS

When you write an essay, it's important to organize your ideas so that you can present them clearly. In English, writers divide or organize ideas into smaller parts or paragraphs to make them easier to understand. Each paragraph then develops and strengthens the writer's main point.

As you know, academic writing follows certain rules and patterns. It is especially important for you, as an academic writer, to follow these rules because your work will be evaluated not only on *what* you write, but also on *how* you write.

Format

You can identify paragraphs in two ways:

1. The first sentence is indented five spaces from the left margin.

OR

2. All the sentences follow the left margin with a space between each paragraph.

Sentences That Form a Paragraph

Academic paragraphs are about *one* topic and *one* main idea about the topic. The main idea, sometimes called the controlling idea, is the point the writer wants to make about the topic. Sometimes, it is the writer's own opinion about the topic.

A **topic sentence** is usually at the beginning of the first paragraph of a passage, but it can also be at the end. This sentence introduces the topic and main idea. A topic alone does not express an idea or opinion. For example, "cycling" is a topic, but "Having a bicycle in the city is better than owning a car" expresses an opinion. Topic sentences must include both parts—the topic and the main idea.

Example:

Academic cheating has recently become more common in high schools and universities,
(topic)

especially because of the ease with which students can copy information from the Internet.
(main idea)

> **Note:** Sometimes there is no topic sentence because the main point is obvious or can be inferred from the details given in other sentences.

Supporting sentences are all the other sentences in the paragraph. All the supporting sentences must relate to the main idea.

Example:

Some Web sites even offer prewritten reports on any topic, which can be purchased for a fee.

Supporting details develop the specific points the writer wants to make about the topic.

Supporting details may include . . .

explanations or illustrations	descriptions
examples	personal experiences
facts or statistics	expert opinions
anecdotes	

Example:

One study showed that one in four students has copied information from the Internet and turned it in as his or her own work.

The **concluding sentence** comes at the end of the paragraph and summarizes or restates the main idea or the opinion of the writer.

Example:

The Internet is a valuable academic research tool; however, without proper monitoring by teachers, it can make it easier for some students to cheat.

EXERCISE 1

A. *Work with another student. Read the paragraph. Which features does it include from the list in the Warm Up?*

Plagiarism, the act of using someone's words or ideas as your own, has become a big problem, and schools are looking for solutions to decrease its occurrence. One solution they have found is a software program that can identify plagiarized text. Students submit their papers electronically, and the software checks the sentences and finds any that have been copied. Some Web sites, like turnitin.com™, offer this service online for a fee. Another way schools have been fighting the problem is to conduct training sessions that teach students about what plagiarism is and how it can be prevented. Schools are hoping that some of these solutions will discourage students from committing this form of academic cheating.

B. *On your own, follow these instructions:*
- Circle where the paragraph is indented.
- Underline the topic sentence.
- Put a star (✱) next to a supporting sentence.
- Write one supporting detail here: _____
- Double underline the concluding sentence.

C. *Compare your work with your partner from Exercise A. Discuss any differences.*

A. *Read the topic sentences. Write the topic and the main idea for each one.*

Topic sentence 1: Commuting to work on the bus is the most relaxing time of my day.

Topic: _____

Main idea: _____

Topic sentence 2: Volunteering at a homeless shelter resulted in opening my eyes in more ways than one.

Topic: _____

Main idea: _____

Topic sentence 3: Although ballet dancers and football players seem very different, they are more alike than you would think.

Topic: _____

Main idea: _____

B. *Compare answers with another student. Discuss any differences.*

A. *Write a topic sentence for each of these topics. Remember to include a main idea.*

1. Good advice from a parent or a teacher: _____

    _____

2. One school rule you would like to change: _____

    _____

3. A hero: _____

    _____

4. One of your personality traits: _____

    _____

5. The reason you study English: _____

    _____

6. Your idea of success: _____

    _____

B. *Share your topic sentences with another student. Identify the main ideas in your partner's sentences.*

Unity

A well-written paragraph is unified. This means all the sentences in a paragraph relate to and support one main idea. Sentences, information, or details that do not relate to the main idea are called "irrelevant." They do not belong in the paragraph.

Example:

    Plagiarism, the act of using someone's words or ideas as your own, has become a big problem, and schools are looking for solutions to decrease its occurrence. One solution they have found is a software program that can identify plagiarized text. Students submit their papers electronically, and the software reads the sentences and finds any that have been copied. Some Web sites, like turnitin.com™, offer this service online for a fee. Turnitin.com™ also offers proofreading and grading services. Another way schools have been fighting the problem is to conduct training sessions that teach students about what plagiarism is and how it can be prevented. Schools are hoping that some of these solutions will discourage students from committing this form of academic cheating.

The highlighted sentence *Turnitin.com™ also offers proofreading and grading services* is not related to the main idea of the paragraph. It is irrelevant information and should not be included.

EXERCISE 4

Read the paragraphs. Write the topic and the main idea for each one. Then underline the irrelevant sentence.

Paragraph 1

    Commuting to work on the bus has become the most relaxing time of the day for me. On the bus, you are not distracted or interrupted like you would be at home or work. At home or at work there are always calls to answer or chores to do. On the bus, everyone is quiet and respects each other's space. The seats are cushioned, and each person has his or her own reading light. Best of all, the time is all yours, and you can listen to music, read a book or newspaper, or sleep. Taking public transportation can also reduce car repair costs and greenhouse gases. Commuting by bus has become one of the most enjoyable parts of my day.

Topic: _____

Main idea: _____

(continued)

Paragraph 2

Many people do not realize how easy and inexpensive it is to exercise at home. You can just turn on the television and check the program listings for the numerous yoga, aerobics, Pilates, or Zumba programs. If you are not home when they are on, you can record them and play them when your schedule allows. Cable television offers hundreds of other channels that show movies, cooking shows, and news programs 24 hours a day. You can also check the Internet for video clips of exercise routines and then bookmark them for repeated use. Moreover, the Internet is a great resource for photos and printouts of exercise plans you can follow.

Topic: _____

Main idea: _____

Paragraph 3

Annika Sorenstam, the world-class golf champion who was ranked as the number one player in 2006, has launched two junior golf programs to help young female golfers attain their athletic potential. Another great golfer, Lorena Ochoa, became the number one player in 2007. One of the programs, the Annika Cup, invites young female Swedish competitors to play together on teams in a golf tournament. Because golf is usually a solo sport, players learn how to work together to reach a goal. The second program, which began in 2003 when Annika began working with the Swedish Golf Federation, helps young female players stay strong academically and competitively to win scholarships for college.

Topic: _____

Main idea: _____

A. *Choose one of your topic sentences from Exercise 3. Use it to write a paragraph on a separate piece of paper.*

B. *Exchange paragraphs with a partner. Answer these questions about your partner's paragraph. Then discuss the questions with your partner.*

- What is the topic? _____

- What is the main idea? _____

- Are all the sentences connected to the main idea? If not, which ones are irrelevant?

  _____

  _____

  _____

Paragraph Types

Every paragraph has a purpose. For example, it may define special terms, explain a process, or show cause and effect. Choosing the appropriate paragraph type will focus your ideas and help your readers understand and remember your main point.

There are several paragraph types, including:

Process/Sequence—explains a process, steps, or series of events, for example, *how volcanoes are formed* or *the building of the Taj Mahal*

Cause/Effect—shows how someone or something makes something happen, or how something changes something or someone, for example *What are the causes of lung cancer? How does stress affect health?*

Comparison—shows how two things or people are similar or different, for example *How are the rules of baseball and cricket different?*

Definition—describes something and its special characteristics, for example *What is a dwarf planet?* or *What is a socially responsible company?*

Problem/Solution—explains a problem and a possible way or ways to solve the problem, like *how to prevent academic cheating* or *how to solve a problem at work*.

Transitions and Signal Words

In each paragraph type, writers often use certain key words and phrases, called transitions (or signal words), to organize the paragraph.

EXERCISE 6

Read the chart. Circle the transitions you have used in your writing. Then compare them with another student.

Paragraph Patterns	Transitions for Organizing Paragraphs
Process/Sequence	**Sequence expressions:** The first step, second, third next, then, finally before, when, during, after, once, as soon as **Dates or years:** On October 6, 1926, . . . In 1919, . . . **Ages:** When she was fourteen, . . .
Cause/Effect	causes / resulted in makes / produces is caused by / is a result of / is due to consequently / therefore because / so / thus
Comparison	both / same / alike / similar to different from On one hand . . . / On the other hand . . .
Definition	be (is, are), seem / consist of is defined as . . . This means . . .
Problem/Solution	A common problem / issue / dilemma . . . A solution . . . Another idea / way . . . resolve / need / solve

EXERCISE 7

Read each paragraph. Then write the paragraph type and transitions the writer used.

Paragraph 1

These are some basic steps you need to remember before you hit the golf ball. The first step, and what most pros will tell you, is to check your grip on the club. A bad grip will always throw the ball off line. The second basic step is your stance. With your feet hip-width apart, check that there is a parallel line that travels across your toes and extends in the direction you want your ball to travel. Next, look at the target as a hunter would its prey. Finally, look at the ball, keep your head down, and swing. If you follow these simple fundamentals, you are likely to see the benefits on your score card.

Paragraph type: _____

Transitions: _____

Paragraph 2

Volunteering at a homeless shelter resulted in opening my eyes in more ways than one. I was a very fortunate teenager, living comfortably in a big, beautiful home with plenty of food and two loving parents who took good care of me. One day, my mother, who had started a homeless shelter, "volunteered" me because she needed more help. I was not very happy about having to go; I was more interested in being with my friends or watching television. On that bitterly cold night when we got to the shelter, there were 25 to 30 people waiting to come in. They wore tattered scarves and hats, so it was difficult to make out their faces. After everyone came inside, my job was easy. I just had to help serve a hot meal and distribute clean blankets. This seemed simple enough until my mom asked me to sit down at the table and join the shelter guests. At first, I felt very uncomfortable, even nervous of our guests, but then some of the guests asked me what my name was, where I went to school, and what I liked to do. Our guests were making me feel at home. Over our dinner I got to know their stories as well. I learned about a way of life I knew nothing about—life with no money, no food, and little hope. As a result of listening to their lives of hardship, I came to realize in a very personal way that life was not kind to everyone and circumstances and personality can sometimes make us powerless. This became one of many nights I spent at the shelter. Little did I know how giving a few hours of my time to help others would change me.

Paragraph type: _____

Transitions: _____

(continued)

Paragraph 3

Although ballet dancers and football players seem very different, they are, in fact, more alike than you would think. Both dancers and players must keep to a rigorous training schedule. They must be highly disciplined to endure the long hours every day in the ballet studio or gym doing exercises to build their strength and agility. They tirelessly practice drills and routines with special patterns in preparation for the day they will perform for their audiences. Another similarity is the equipment they use. Football players wear special shoes with cleats on the soles that grip the ground so they can move more easily. Ballet dancers wear soft-soled shoes or pointe shoes that they cover with rosin, a sticky powder, which allows them to glide gracefully on the dance floor without slipping. Like dancers, football players use leg wear that is stretchy so that they can run, jump, and extend their legs. Lastly, in terms of athletic ability, they need to have great flexibility, balance, power, and specially trained muscles. When you consider the artist and sports player, they are both highly-skilled, specialized athletes.

Paragraph type: _____

Transitions: _____

Paragraph 4

According to a recent survey conducted by the Josephson Institute (2008), academic cheating is a growing problem. One way colleges and universities are trying to address this situation is by creating programs that aim to deter students from cheating. Some colleges are instituting an honor code or contract that students promise to follow. Another idea colleges are trying is to enlist peers to participate in campaigns to discourage cheating with slogans like "Honesty is the best policy." Furthermore, students who are caught cheating are not always expelled, but may be required to attend counseling programs that help students understand and change their behavior. These are just a few measures schools are taking to keep students on the right path.

Paragraph type: _____

Transitions: _____

EXERCISE 8

A. *Choose one of these topics and write a paragraph on a separate piece of paper. Before you write, decide which paragraph type fits your topic. Use appropriate transitions and signal words.*

- A time when you helped someone
- Two of your closest friends
- How to become more self-confident
- What being responsible means to you

B. *Exchange paragraphs with another student. Answer these questions about your partner's paragraph. Then discuss them with your partner.*

- What is the paragraph type? _____

- What are some transitions or signal words that identify the paragraph type?

_____

- Are there any other transition words or phrases the writer could add? What are they?

_____

Supporting Details

> "It's the little details that are vital. Little things make big things happen."
>
> –John Wooden (University of California basketball coach)

A paragraph can have a topic sentence and a purpose, but without enough details, the reader will be unable to fully understand the topic. Writers need to organize their paragraphs in a way that strengthens and clarifies the main idea. Supporting details bring ideas to life.

Supporting details may include:

explanations or illustrations to give reasons why something happened, or describe how something works—*Students may be cheating more because cell phones make it easier.*

examples to show what you mean or what something is like—*An example of academic cheating is plagiarism.*

facts or statistics to strengthen a point and provide evidence—*According to the Pew Internet and American Life Project (2011), 77 percent of teens who have cell phones bring them to school every day.*

anecdotes, which are short interesting stories about a particular person or event. They can help emphasize or clarify the main idea.

descriptions to give details about what someone or something is like—*The student was agitated and suddenly exploded with anger, which was unlike him.*

personal experiences to connect the writer's experience to the main idea to make it easier to understand

expert opinions, including opinions and quotations from people with special skills or knowledge, to support the main idea

A. *Work with another student. Look back at Exercise 7. Find a supporting detail sentence from each paragraph and write it below. Then write the type of supporting detail from the box. (More than one answer may be possible.)*

anecdote	expert opinion	fact or statistic
description	explanation or illustration	personal experience
example		

Paragraph 1

Supporting detail: _____

Type: _____

Paragraph 2

Supporting detail: _____

Type: _____

Paragraph 3

Supporting detail: _____

Type: _____

Paragraph 4

Supporting detail: _____

Type: _____

B. *Share your answers with the class.*

WRITING TASK

Write a paragraph that includes all the elements of a good academic paragraph.

A. *Which of these topics are you interested in writing about? Which one do you know the most about? Choose one topic and write it at the top of a separate piece of paper.*

- A person of integrity
- A great athlete or sport
- The most challenging thing I have tried to do
- My greatest success or failure
- How I learned to . . .
- A problem I solved

Example:

> The most challenging thing I have tried to do: learn hip-hop dancing

B. *On your paper, brainstorm some notes about your topic. To help you think of details, ask and answer Wh- questions about your experience with the topic: Who . . . ? What . . . ? Where . . . ? When . . . ? Why . . . ? How . . . ? (See the example below.)*

C. *Review your brainstorm and decide which details are the most important for your topic. Cross out any details that are not directly related to your main idea.*

Example:

> What was it?
> a hip-hop class
>
> When did it happen?
> when I was in high school from 12:00 to 1:30 p.m. on Mondays and Wednesdays
>
> Where did it happen?
> ~~at a performing arts school~~
> City Dance Studio
> ~~Minneapolis, Minnesota~~
>
> Why was it challenging?
> - took me a long time to learn what the teacher wanted me to do
> - felt silly trying to do the steps and final routine
> - was a beginner
> - ~~had to quickly memorize dance routines~~
>
> How did the experience affect me?
> - learned not to give up
> - learned to not worry about what others think

D. *Choose the paragraph type that best expresses your main idea.*

> process/sequence   compare/contrast   problem/solution
> cause/effect   definition

E. *On a new piece of paper, write a topic sentence. Remember to include your main idea as part of the sentence.*

Example:

Learning how to hip-hop dance taught me some important life lessons.

F. *Write your paragraph. Follow the guidelines and skills introduced in this unit:*

- indented first line of the paragraph
- topic sentence that introduces one topic and one main idea
- supporting sentences that all connect to the main idea
- adequate support and details

Check Your Writing

A. *Use this form to check your own paragraph, or exchange paragraphs with another student and check each other's writing.*

Academic Paragraph Checklist

The paragraph . . .

1. is indented. ☐

2. has a topic sentence that introduces the topic and one main idea. ☐

3. has supporting sentences that all connect to the main idea. ☐

4. includes supporting details. ☐

5. follows one of the paragraph patterns from this unit. ☐

6. has a concluding sentence that summarizes or restates the main idea. ☐

7. Were there any irrelevant sentences or information? If so, write a question mark (?) in front of them on the paragraph.

8. Underline any transitions from the unit that are used in the paragraph.

9. What changes do you suggest to improve the paragraph?

_____

_____

_____

_____

_____

B. *Make changes to improve your paragraph. Remember to check your writing for grammar, spelling, and punctuation errors.*

Summary Writing

Being able to write a good summary is one of the most important skills for school and beyond. Academic writing assignments often include summaries of important ideas from source materials such as textbooks, Web sites, and lectures.

Writing summaries helps you to review and reinforce the information you are learning.

This unit will help you learn to decide which information to include and how to write a clear, concise summary.

Warm Up

Work in a group. Choose one of these topics. Answer the question, "What was it about?"

- The last movie you saw or your favorite movie
- The last book you read or your favorite book
- The last television show you watched or your favorite television show

GOOD SUMMARIES

A good summary includes just enough information—not too much and not too little. It gives the main idea, information about the point of view or opinions expressed, and just a few details and examples to support those points.

Guidelines for Writing Summaries

A good summary . . .

- is shorter than the original text

- only includes the main ideas

- does not include small, unimportant details

- is written in your own words (though you may use important expressions or terms from the original)

- does not include exact full sentences from the original

- includes a reference to the original source

- does not include new ideas or your own opinion

EXERCISE 1

Work with another student. Write the "Do's" and "Don'ts" for summary writing in the correct columns in the chart.

copy full sentences from the original text

include only the main ideas

use your own words

keep it short

include your own opinion

include a reference to the original source

include small details

include new ideas

use key words, terms, or quotations if necessary

Do	Don't

A Summary of a Story or Event—What Is It About?

For academic writing, you may need to summarize stories and events for various purposes, for example, for exam questions, essays, and research papers.

When you retell a story or event, you focus on the main idea and the plot—on what happened. The plot is the important moments that keep the story moving.

Useful Phrases for Story Summaries	
(Title) is a story / book by (author).	Suddenly, . . .
(Title) tells the story of . . .	One day / evening . . .
The story is about . . .	The next day . . .
In the story . . .	Hours / Months / Years later, . . .
The main character is . . .	Meanwhile . . .
As the story begins, . . .	However, . . .
During . . .	At this point . . .
While . . .	To his surprise . . .
Before long . . .	To make matters even worse . . .
Soon . . .	Eventually, . . . / Finally, . . .
As soon as . . .	

EXERCISE 2

A. *Read this famous fable from Aesop called "The Boy Who Cried Wolf."*

The Boy Who Cried Wolf
An Aesop Fable

A long time ago, there was a little shepherd boy who lived in a small village near a field. Every day, it was his job to take the sheep out to the field and watch and protect them. His days were long, and there was no one to talk to or play with. He often felt bored and lonely. No one from the village ever came out to the field to spend time with him because they were always busy doing their work. One especially boring day, the boy got an idea. He cried out loudly, "Help, help! There's a wolf!" The villagers heard his cries and immediately stopped what they were doing and rushed to the field to help the boy. The lonely boy was very happy to see so many villagers. When the villagers arrived, they were surprised to find that there was no wolf. The boy had played a nasty trick. They scolded the boy and told him not to cry "Wolf!" if there was no wolf.

The next day, once again, the boy became bored and lonely. He thought about what the villagers had said, but soon his thoughts turned to how alone he felt, so he cried out again, "Help, help! There's a wolf!" Again the busy villagers stopped their work and ran quickly to the field. When they discovered the boy had pretended again that there was a wolf, they warned him to *never* again cry "Wolf!" if there was no wolf. "You must only call for help if there is really a wolf," they said.

The next day, the boy was sitting under a tree and watching his sheep when a real wolf appeared! Frightened, the boy yelled as loudly as he could "Help! Please help me! A wolf is attacking the sheep!" But this time the villagers did not pay any attention to his cries. "Does he think we are fools? He's just pretending again," they said.

After losing all of his sheep to the wolf, the boy returned to the village to face his neighbors. That day the boy learned that nobody believes a liar . . . even when he's telling the truth!

B. *Read a student's summary of "The Boy Who Cried Wolf."*

> "The Boy Who Cried Wolf" by Aesop is a fable that teaches the importance of telling the truth. In the story, a boy is watching his sheep. He is bored and lonely and wants some company, so he cries, "Wolf!" The townspeople come to help him, but find no wolf. They scold him and tell him not to do that again. The next day, however, the boy cries "Wolf!" again, and the people come back. When they find no wolf again, they become very angry. Finally, when a real wolf appears the boy cries for help again, but the villagers do not come because they think he is lying, so the wolf eats the sheep. The boy learns that "nobody believes a liar . . . even when he's telling the truth!"

C. *Work with another student. Discuss these questions:*

- How does the length of the original fable compare to the summary?
- In the summary, where is the reference to the original story and author?
- Where in the summary is the main idea mentioned?
- Which details from the original are not included in the summary?
- Which key terms or quotations from the original are used in the summary?

A. *Prepare to write your own summary of the folktale "The Emperor and the Seed." Follow these steps:*

1. Preview the original text:
   - Read the title and the first paragraph. (See Part 3, Unit 4 for more on previewing.)

2. Identify the main idea:
   - Read the text.
   - Check the meanings of any words you need to understand the main idea.
   - Underline key words and phrases that relate to the main point of the story.

3. Identify important information or examples that support the main idea.
   - Mark them with a "✱"

4. Decide which information is not important.

The Emperor and the Seed

Once there was an emperor of India. The emperor was very old, and he knew it was time to choose the new emperor. In the old tradition, the emperor chose one of his own children to be the next leader, but this emperor did something different. He called all the young people together. He said, "It is time to choose the next emperor, and I am going to choose one of you."

The children could not believe these words. The emperor continued, "I am going to give each of you one seed today—a very special seed. I want you to plant the seed, water it, and put it in the sun. Come back here one year from today and show me what you grew. I will check each of your plants, and the one I choose will be the next emperor!"

A boy named Arun was there that day, and he received a seed from the emperor. He ran home and told his mother the story. She helped Arun get a pot, and he planted the seed and watered it carefully. Every day he checked to see if his plant grew, but after several weeks, still nothing grew in the pot. Now all the children in the village were talking about their plants, but Arun didn't have a plant. He wondered, "Why did I fail? Did I give the seed too much water, or was the sun too hot?" Arun waited and waited for his seed to grow, but it did not. Not even a small plant grew.

Finally, one year passed, and all the youths brought their plants to the emperor. Arun asked his mother, "Can I really go before the emperor with an empty pot, or should I stay home and forget this stupid contest?"

Arun's mother said, "Arun, you must be honest. Go and take your empty pot. The emperor is waiting."

Arun knew his mother was right. When he arrived, he saw all the beautiful plants of the other children. He put his empty pot on the floor, and the others laughed at him. When the emperor entered, Arun tried to hide in the back of the room. "What great plants, trees, and flowers you all grew," said the emperor. "Today, one of you will become the next emperor!" Then the emperor saw Arun with his empty pot. He ordered his guards to bring Arun to the front with his pot. Arun was scared. "The emperor knows I failed! He is going to punish me!"

The emperor asked Arun his name. All the children laughed and made fun of Arun. The emperor looked at Arun. Then he said, "Here is your new emperor! His name is Arun!" Arun was shocked. He couldn't grow his seed. How could he be the new emperor?

The emperor explained, "One year ago, I gave you all a seed. I told you to plant the seed, water it, and bring it back to me today. But I gave you all boiled seeds; I knew they would not grow. All of you, except Arun, brought me trees, plants, and flowers. You are not honest. When the first seed did not grow, you planted another seed in your pot. Arun is the only one with the courage and honesty to bring me an empty pot. Arun is the one who will be the new emperor!"

B. *Write a summary of the story on a separate piece of paper. Check the guidelines on page 117.*

C. *Exchange summaries with another student. Does your partner's summary follow the guidelines? How are your summaries the same? How are they different?*

A Summary of a News Article

News articles can be short or long. Depending on what is important in the story, an article may give a lot of detailed information, examples, and quotations. Most news articles answer the following *Wh-* questions:

- *Who* is involved in the story?
- *What* happened?
- *When* did it happen?
- *Where* did it happen?
- *Why* did it happen?
- *How* did it happen?

A good summary of a news article will answer the same questions, leaving out unimportant details.

Useful Phrases for News Article Summaries
The article "(Title)" is about . . .
The story focuses on . . .
The story is about . . .
In the article "(Title)," (Author's Name) writes about . . .
The events took place . . .

A. *Read the article about U.S. cyclist Floyd Landis.*

Cyclist Finally Admits Doping[1]

Floyd Landis, the fallen cycling champion, has finally admitted to taking performance-enhancing[2] drugs. Landis's 2006 Tour de France title was taken away when blood tests showed abnormally high levels of testosterone and erythropoietin, two types of performance enhancers. Landis had previously denied his involvement in doping. Now the athlete admits that he used a number of banned substances while he was competing in races from 2002 to 2006.

From the start of his cycling career, Landis was destined to be one of the best in the sport. He won the first race he entered and became the U.S. junior national champion in 1993. Landis's talent drew the attention of Lance Armstrong, seven-time winner of the Tour de France, who invited Landis to join the U.S. Postal Service team. They rode together as teammates from 2002 to 2004 in the Tour de France. Armstrong won all of these races.

Now Landis's motives for announcing his repeated drug usage are being questioned because he had already lost his title due to earlier positive results from drug testing. Landis claims that after years of lying about his drug use, he wants to tell the truth and clear his conscience. He thinks the world should know that drug cheating was common among competitors, including Armstrong. Armstrong has adamantly denied the accusations, and drug tests he has submitted have come back negative.

[1]*doping*—taking drugs in order to become a stronger, better athlete
[2]*performance-enhancing drugs*—drugs that some athletes use to improve their strength and ability

B. *Work with another student. Read the two summaries. Which one do you think is better? Discuss your lists of* Do's *and* Don'ts *in Exercise 1.*

Summary 1

Landis has finally admitted to taking performance-enhancing drugs like testosterone and erythropoietin. He was always one of the best in the sport and won many races early on. He was the U.S. junior national champion in 1993. He competed alongside Lance Armstrong, the seven-time winner of the Tour de France. Landis won the race in 2006, but lost his title when tests proved he was using illegal drugs.

Summary 2

> In the article "Cyclist Finally Admits Doping," former Tour de France winner Floyd Landis admits he cheated by taking performance enhancing drugs after years of denying it. People are wondering why he made the announcement since he had already lost his Tour de France title and his usage of performance-enhancing drugs was well known. Landis also accused seven-time Tour de France champion Lance Armstrong of doping as well. They were teammates from 2002 to 2004. Armstrong strongly maintains that he has never engaged in doping, and his drug tests have proven it.

EXERCISE 5

A. *Preview the title of the article. What do you think it will be about?*

An Enduring Problem in the Sports World

B. *Skim (read through quickly) the article once. Look up the meanings of any important vocabulary (words you need to know to understand the main idea).*

Dan Caldwell
January 25, 2013

No one really knows when athletes first started relying on performance-enhancing drugs to beat their competitors, but in the 1970s, suspicions started to grow when East German athletes began breaking all kinds of world records. Their victories did not seem due to rigorous training or talent. There was no possibility at that time for the public to find out that the Soviet government (which ruled East Germany at the time) and doctors, coaches, and sports officials fully supported the practice of drug use.

In 1989, the Berlin Wall fell, and so did the "mystery" behind all the wins. East German athletes started telling their tragic stories of government-sponsored doping and the horrible side effects, such as liver damage, infertility, and psychological problems. Since then, the doctors, coaches, and officials have been convicted in the German courts, and athletes have received money for the damage the drugs caused. Of course, nothing can ever heal the pain these athletes suffered.

The revelation of the problems suffered by East German athletes did not lessen the use of performance-enhancing drugs in sports. If athletes feel they cannot win without them, doping will continue to ruin the reputations of those who would have been considered "the greatest" without them. This disgraceful practice is damaging the whole world of sports. Not long ago, people marveled at truly gifted athletes. Now, people question whether today's top athletes are really playing fair.

C. *Read the article again. What is the main idea?*

> ## Remember
>
> When you find new vocabulary words that are useful for your writing, write them in your vocabulary notebook. (See Part 2, Unit 1.)

D. *In the article, underline important information that should be included in a summary. Cross out any details that are not important.*

E. *On a separate piece of paper, write a summary of the article. Begin like this:*

In the article "An Enduring Problem in the Sports World," Dan Caldwell writes about . . .

A Summary for Study Purposes

Study summaries are summaries you write on your own to help you study for a topic, for example, before an exam or before you write a report. Writing this kind of summary after reading an assignment or attending a lecture can help you review class materials and identify important points and information you need to learn.

Useful Phrases for Study Summaries	
The chapter / article / interview / passage is about . . . The study / research showed that . . . The writer discusses . . .	The main points are . . . The writer / speaker gives examples of . . . The speaker argues that . . .

A. *Preview the title of the radio talk show transcript. What do you think will be the main point discussed on the show?*

Winners That Lose

B. *Work with a partner. Preview the vocabulary from the radio talk show interview. Then complete the sentences with the best word or phrase. Change the form of the word if necessary (for example, from singular to plural or present to past tense).*

measure up—to be good enough to do a particular job or to reach a particular standard

emphasis—special importance

side effect—an effect that a drug has on your body in addition to the intended effect

expectation—a feeling or belief about the way something should be or how someone should behave

steroids—a drug to treat illness and injuries; sometimes used illegally by athletes to improve their performance

get away with—to not be noticed or punished when you have done something wrong

tempted—considering doing something bad or wrong

1. My parents hope I will get an athletic scholarship to help pay for college. They have high _____ for me and my future.

2. Sarah experienced bad _____ after she took some medication for a headache.

3. Many young athletes think they can _____ cheating because they read about so many athletes who never get caught.

4. Athletic departments and parents need to put more _____ on how to play sports fairly, even if that means losing.

5. The news has been full of stories about famous athletes who have taken _____ to perform better.

6. John's teammate was getting bigger and stronger. He knew his teammate was taking steroids. John was _____ to do the same.

7. Some young athletes are worried that they will never be able to compete professionally. They feel they will never _____ to the professionals.

C. *Read the radio talk show transcript.*

Host: Good morning, listeners. This is Sherman Jones on "Up to Date." It seems that every week we hear about another great athlete who took illegal drugs to get to the top. And more and more college and high school athletes are following the same course. With us today to talk about why young people are taking the easy way out and why athletes should be aware that winning at all costs can be costly is Pete Andrews, athletic director at Stanton High School in Dallas, Texas. Welcome to our program, Pete.

Pete: Glad to be here.

Host: Why do you think so many teens are tempted to use steroids?

Pete: Well, we live in a super competitive culture. There is a lot of pressure from parents, from schools, and from society to be the best. It seems more emphasis is placed on winning than on playing fairly. Kids might feel that it is impossible to measure up to these expectations. So they see these superhuman, world-class athletes, and they want to be like them. However, they are only seeing the big, powerful bodies, and the wins—not the serious side effects of steroid use.

Host: What are the side effects?

Pete: For young people especially, the side effects are serious. There's hair loss, dizziness, aching joints, stunted growth, nausea or vomiting, high blood pressure, risk of heart failure, just to name a few.

Host: Dangerous stuff!

Pete: And that doesn't count the psychological effects . . . Steroids can make teens moody, irritable, or depressed. Some kids even become combative or aggressive. . . . You know, the sad fact is that they see so many professional athletes get away with it today.

Host: How do you keep young athletes on the right track?

Pete: At our school, we have students and their parents sign a form promising that the students will not use any type of illegal substances. But more importantly, we keep emphasizing the importance of following a basic health regimen—a good night's sleep, exercise, and proper training, and, of course, eating right. Staying healthy helps athletes stay on top. Finally, we emphasize that if you play fair, you'll always be a winner. We remind parents of this, too.

Host: Pete, I want to thank you for stopping by to talk about the challenges facing our schools and young athletes today.

Pete: My pleasure. Thank you.

D. *Check (✓) the statement that best expresses the main idea of the interview.*

_____ Steroids are dangerous and can cause many serious side effects.

_____ Student athletes rationalize their decision to use steroids by thinking about professional athletes who use drugs.

_____ Schools and parents need to lessen the focus on winning and emphasize the importance of health and a good training program to deter students from taking steroids.

E. *Mark each statement T (true) or F (false). Then compare answers with another student.*

_____ **1.** More and more student athletes are using steroids because of the pressure to win.

_____ **2.** Students are usually aware of the dangerous side effects from steroid use.

_____ **3.** Steroids can affect the way young people feel emotionally.

_____ **4.** Student athletes may use professional athletes who use steroids to rationalize their own decision to do the same.

_____ **5.** At Stanton High School, all student athletes must make a promise not to use illegal substances.

_____ **6.** Pete says that winning is the most important thing for athletes.

F. *Write a list of the important information from the interview on a piece of paper. Use your own words. Decide which information is necessary for your summary.*

G. *On a separate piece of paper, write a summary of the interview. Begin like this:*

> *On the radio show "Up to Date," Sherman Jones interviews a high school athletic director about . . .*

Write a Biographical Summary

Biographical profiles (the story of a person's life) are commonly found in textbooks, articles, and reports. You may need to write a biography when you are studying an important or influential person, such as an author, artist, or politician, or when you interview someone for a class report.

Biographical summaries usually follow a chronological pattern.

Useful Phrases for Biographical Summaries	
(Name) was born in . . .	Between the years of X and Y . . .
In his / her early life, . . .	After beginning / moving to / graduating from / finishing . . .
When he / she was (age), . . .	It was then that he / she . . .
During this period, he / she . . .	Later . . .
At that time, . . .	At one point . . .

A. *Preview the title of the online article. What do you think you will learn about Dr. Paul Farmer?*

Dr. Paul Farmer—Man of Compassion and Integrity, Part 1, 1959–1999

B. *Preview the vocabulary in the box. Underline any words you do not know.*

anthropology	disable	houseboat	unconventional
creek	hardships	rural	upbringing

C. *Work with another student. Discuss the meanings of the vocabulary. Look up any words you both do not know.*

D. *Read the article.*

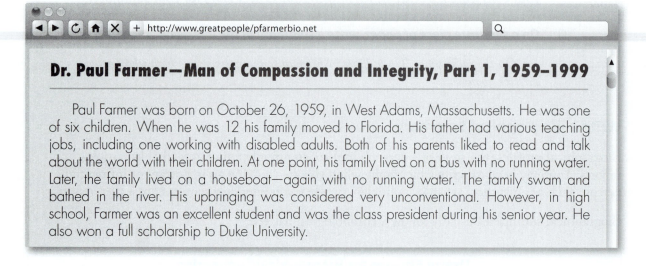

Dr. Paul Farmer—Man of Compassion and Integrity, Part 1, 1959–1999

Paul Farmer was born on October 26, 1959, in West Adams, Massachusetts. He was one of six children. When he was 12 his family moved to Florida. His father had various teaching jobs, including one working with disabled adults. Both of his parents liked to read and talk about the world with their children. At one point, his family lived on a bus with no running water. Later, the family lived on a houseboat—again with no running water. The family swam and bathed in the river. His upbringing was considered very unconventional. However, in high school, Farmer was an excellent student and was the class president during his senior year. He also won a full scholarship to Duke University.

During his years at Duke, Farmer studied science and anthropology and met and read about people who would influence his later work. As an undergraduate, he became familiar with the writings of Rudolf Virchow, a nineteenth century German physician who looked at culture, health, politics, and anthropology, and envisioned the first public healthcare system. He also met Haitian migrant workers who lived and worked near the Duke campus and learned of the terrible poverty and living conditions they suffered in their home country as well as the hardships they faced in the United States. It was during his conversations with the Haitian migrants that he picked up their language, Creole. Farmer also became influenced by religious teachings that emphasized the need to care for those who were less fortunate. In 1982, Paul received his bachelor's degree in medical anthropology. Medical anthropology links the study of health, diseases, and biology, and the influence of culture and society on health and health care programs.

After graduating from Duke, Farmer decided to apply to Harvard Medical School because it offered a dual program in medicine and anthropology. While waiting to hear from Harvard about his application, he traveled to Haiti where he wanted to learn more about the people and the living conditions. Once he arrived, he went out into the rural areas and found that the people had no public services including drinking water, education, or healthcare. There were only a few healthcare workers in those areas, and the training they had received was inadequate. It was then that Farmer realized his mission—to help the poor and sick and provide proper training for health workers. He decided to build a clinic in Haiti. At the same time, Farmer found out that he had been accepted into the program at Harvard University. Farmer traveled back and forth between Harvard and Haiti while he completed his medical degree and a doctorate in anthropology. In the meantime, his clinic grew into a community–based health program called Zanmi Lasante, which eventually provided medical treatment, schools, sanitation, and social services to thousands of Haitians and greatly improved their living conditions.

E. ***Work with another student. Discuss these questions. Do not look back at the article.***

- What are some of Paul Farmer's personal characteristics?
- What people or ideas influenced Paul Farmer?
- What are some of his major achievements?
- What is his philosophy?
- What is the main idea of the article?

F. ***Write down the important information about Paul Farmer on a separate piece of paper. Use your own words. Decide which information is important to include in your summary.***

G. ***On a separate piece of paper, write a summary of Paul Farmer's biography.***

Further Practice

Research and Write/Journal or Blog Topic *(See Part 1, Units 1 and 2.)*

- Interview a classmate about his or her life. Then write a biographical summary of three to four paragraphs.

WRITING TASK

Write a summary about a text of your choice.

A. **Choose one of these types of texts. It can be a text you have already read, or you may choose a new text for this writing task.**
- A short fiction story
- A recent story from the newspaper or from a news website
- A passage from a textbook
- A biography of an interesting person

B. **Read (or reread) the text. Then write a summary using useful phrases and vocabulary from this unit. Follow the guidelines on page 117.**

Check Your Writing

A. **Use this form to check your own summary, or exchange summaries with another student and check each other's writing. If you work with another student, give your partner your summary and a copy of the original text.**

Summary Checklist

The summary . . .

1. is shorter than the original text. ☐

2. only includes the main ideas. ☐

3. does not include small, unimportant details. ☐

4. does not use exact, full sentences from the original text. ☐

5. includes a reference to the original text. ☐

6. Were there any sentences you didn't understand? If so, write a question mark (?) in front of them on the summary.

7. Underline any useful phrases from the unit that are used in the summary.

8. What changes do you suggest to improve the summary?

_____

_____

_____

B. **Make changes to improve your summary. Remember to check your writing for grammar, spelling, and punctuation errors.**

UNIT 4

Working with Source Materials

In colleges and universities, writing plays an important part in helping students gain a deeper understanding of their academic subjects. Teachers often assign essays or other writing assignments to give students a chance to demonstrate their knowledge as well as to express their own opinions and ideas. For longer papers and essays, writing topics generally focus on social, cultural, or scientific issues rather than personal experiences like "My Favorite Vacation" or "My Family" or "How I Spent My Weekend." However, personal experiences may be used to provide support for ideas or opinions.

To build knowledge and analyze topics of study, students use different types of source materials, such as books, websites, magazines, newspapers, TV news reports, movies, interview transcripts, plays, or paintings.

Warm Up

A. *Check (✓) the source materials you have used in your studies. Then write the subjects or topics you studied with each source.*

Sources	Subjects you studied with the sources
☑ textbooks	*history, business, English*
☐ business or government reports	
☐ interviews	
☐ lectures	
☐ magazines or journals	
☐ movies or DVDs	
☐ newspapers	
☐ novels	
☐ research papers	
☐ television or radio transcripts	
☐ websites	

B. *Compare lists with another student. Which sources have you used the most?*

USING SOURCE MATERIALS

Often, your teacher will provide you with source materials for topics you are studying. These materials are usually the starting point for learning new information that you will need for your writing assignments. You may be surprised to discover different aspects or perspectives related to your topic; for example, the historical period, a psychological perspective, or related art movement. Exploring these aspects will help you broaden your knowledge so that you can express yourself more thoughtfully and intelligently about your topic.

EXERCISE 1

A. *Read about one student's experience using source materials.*

One of my favorite subjects in school was acting class. I took the course because a classmate had told me it was an easy way to fulfill a course requirement I needed to graduate. At first, I had no idea what was involved when an actor played a role. I had never wanted to be an actor, but I liked to watch movies on television and thought that acting looked easy.

All that changed over the first few weeks of the class. One of the first things I had to do for the class was to read and analyze a whole play. The professor told us that actors had to know everything about the story and the character they were going to portray, so I had to study the script and learn what the story was about. I did not just learn the lines my character had to say in the play. I had to understand the structure of a comedy play and decide why each character behaved in certain ways. To fully understand the play and characters, I also had to learn all about the time in history when the play took place. I went to the library and looked at history books, and I found more information on the Internet. My teacher also made us go to a museum to look at paintings of people who had lived during that time so we could study their clothing, lifestyles, and gestures. The script, the paintings, and the extra reading all helped me understand who my character was and why the play was important.

By the time we performed the play, I had learned a lot about history, architecture, and human lifestyles and behavior. And I had thought this class was going to be easy!

B. *Work in a group. Discuss these questions:*

- What subject was the student studying?
- What kinds of sources did the student use?
- What did the student learn from the sources?

EXERCISE 2

A. *Do a ten-to-fifteen-minute freewrite about an experience when you used source materials, either for school or for your own interests. Answer these questions:*

- What were you studying?
- What types of materials did you use?
- What did you learn?
- What challenges did you have?

B. *Share your experiences with a partner. How were they the same? How were they different?*

UNDERSTANDING AND ANALYZING SOURCE MATERIALS

Being able to understand and analyze source materials is essential for academic success. Learning something new is often challenging. Researchers have found that it is helpful to connect what you are studying to something you already know about. Thinking about your own experiences, knowledge, and opinions about a topic is one strategy that can help you understand source materials.

Other useful strategies include:

- Previewing
- Underlining, highlighting, and taking notes
- Answering or creating study questions
- Writing a first-response journal
- Building your vocabulary (See Part 2, Unit 1)

In the next section, you will practice strategies to understand and analyze source materials on the topics of personality type, honesty and dishonesty, and academic cheating.

Previewing

A preview gives you a general idea of what something (for example a book or a movie) is about. Think about movie previews. They tell you if the movie is going to be a comedy, a drama, a thriller, or an action film. They introduce the characters and the main point of the story. While you are watching, you may think either, "I know what this is going to be about" or "This is new. I've never seen this before."

In the same way, for your academic studies, previewing source materials will help you understand what each source is about and how useful it will be for your studies. Previewing will also help you start connecting what you already know to what you are about to learn and write about.

Titles

One way to preview a topic is to look at the titles and section headings of the source material. This might be a textbook chapter, an article, a movie review, or lecture transcript. Asking yourself a few questions about the lesson topic can help you think about the information you will learn.

EXERCISE 3

A. *Read these titles from assigned articles, units, and lectures for a university psychology course. Below each one, write any unknown vocabulary words from the title. Look up the words and write their meanings. Then write your answers to the questions.*

1. "Winning Wrongly: A Big Loss for Athletes"

   Vocabulary and meanings: _____

   _____

   What do you think the article is going to be about? _____

   What are one or two things you already know about the topic? _____

   _____

2. "Sharing Music Files: Right or Wrong?"

   Vocabulary and meanings: _____

   _____

   What do you think the article is going to be about? _____

   What are one or two things you already know about the topic? _____

   _____

3. "More MBA Students Cheating to Graduate"

   Vocabulary and meanings: _____

   _____

   What do you think the article is going to be about? _____

   What are one or two things you already know about the topic? _____

   _____

4. "Unit 7: Theories of Personality"

Vocabulary and meanings: _____

_____

What do you think the unit is going to be about? _____

What are one or two things you already know about the topic? _____

_____

5. "Personality Traits and Dishonesty"

Vocabulary and meanings: _____

_____

What do you think the article is going to be about? _____

What are one or two things you already know about the topic? _____

_____

B. *Compare answers with another student.*

C. *Add any new vocabulary words to your vocabulary notebook. (See Part 2, Unit 1.)*

Headings, Images, and Sidebars

When you preview source materials, in addition to titles, take a few minutes to read the headings (the titles written in bold before each section) and skim some of the first sentences of the paragraphs. If there are photos or other images, make sure to look at them, too. As the saying goes, "A picture is worth a thousand words."

Guidelines for Previewing Source Material

These quick strategies will help you understand the main idea and make connections to the topic:

- Read the title and think about the topic.

- Look at images or photographs. Read the *captions* (words under the images). Images will activate what you already know or will learn about the topic.

- Read quotations or text in boxes or margins, called *sidebars*. These usually highlight important ideas.

- Read the headings and other bold words in the text. This will help you prepare for what you are going to learn.

- Read the first sentence after each heading.

- Ask yourself, "What do I already know about this topic? What do I want / need to know?"

A. *Work with another student. Preview the article. Follow these steps:*

1. Read the title. What do you think the article will be about? What are one or two things that you already know about the topic?

2. Look at the photograph. Does it tell you any additional information about the topic?

3. Read the quote in the sidebar. What does it tell you about the topic? What is your reaction to the information? Explain.

4. Read the four headings (bold text). What do you think you will find out in each section?

5. Read the first sentence under each heading. What more do you want to know?

http://research.news.study/net

Study Examines the Psychology Behind Students Who Don't Cheat

Research News (Aug. 18)—While many studies have examined cheating among college students, new research looks at the issue from a different perspective[1]–identifying students who are *least* likely to cheat.

Traits Stand Out[2]

The study of students at one Ohio university found that students who scored high on measures of courage, empathy[3] and honesty were less likely than others to report their cheating in the past—or their intentions to cheat in the future.

Moreover, those students who reported less cheating were also less likely to believe that their fellow students regularly committed academic dishonesty.

People who don't cheat "have a more positive view of others," said Sara Staats, coauthor of the research and professor of psychology at Ohio State University's Newark campus.

Clues to Cheating Behavior

In contrast, those who scored lower on courage, empathy, and honesty—and who are more likely to report that they have cheated—see other students as cheating much more often than they do, rationalizing[4] their own behavior, Staats said.

The issue is important because most recent studies suggest cheating is common on college campuses. Typically, more than half—and sometimes up to 80 percent—of college students report that they have cheated.

Academic Heroes

Staats said this continuing research project aimed to find out more about the students who don't cheat. "Students who don't cheat seem to be in the minority[5], and have plenty of opportunities to see their peers cheat and receive the rewards with little risk of punishment," Staats said. "We see avoiding cheating as a form of everyday heroism[6] in an academic setting."

> People who don't cheat " have a more positive view of others. "

The students completed measures that examined their bravery, honesty and empathy. The researchers separated those who scored in the top half of those measures and contrasted them with those in the bottom half.

Those who scored in the top half—whom the researchers called "academic heroes"—were less likely to have reported cheating in the past 30 days and the last year compared to those in the bottom half. They also indicated they would be less likely to cheat in the next 30 days in one of their classes. The academic heroes also reported they would feel more guilt if they cheated compared to nonheroes.

"The heroes didn't rationalize cheating the way others did, they didn't come up with excuses and say it was OK because lots of other students were doing it," Staats said.

Targeting "Uncertain" Cheaters

Staats said one reason to study cheating at colleges and universities is to try to figure out ways to reduce academic dishonesty. The results from this research suggest a good target audience for anti-cheating messages.

When the researchers asked students if they intended to cheat in the future, nearly half—47 percent—said they did not intend to cheat, but nearly one in four agreed or strongly agreed that they would cheat.

The remaining 29 percent indicated that they were uncertain whether or not they would cheat.

"These 29 percent are like undecided voters—they would be an especially good focus for intervention[7]," Staats said. "Our results suggest that interventions may have a real opportunity to influence at least a quarter of the student population."

Staats said more work needs to be done to identify the best ways to prevent cheating. But this research, with its focus on positive psychology, suggests one avenue, she said.

"We need to do more to recognize integrity[8] among our students, and find ways to tap into[9] the bravery, honesty, and empathy that was found in the academic heroes in our study," she said.

[1]*perspective*—an opinion or view of something

[2]*stand out*—to be very easy to see or notice

[3]*empathy*—the ability to understand someone else's feelings and problems

[4]*rationalize*—to give reasons to explain or excuse one's bad behavior

[5]*be in the minority*—to be less in number than any other group

[6]*heroism*—very great courage

[7]*intervention*—the act of trying to do something to try to stop an argument, problem, war, etc.

[8]*integrity*—the quality of being honest and having high moral principles

[9]*tap into*—to use or take what you need from a supply of something

B. **Read the article. Then, with the class, discuss how the previewing steps helped you understand the article.**

Underlining, Highlighting, and Notetaking

Whenever you read or listen to something, you try to figure out what it is about. Identifying the main ideas helps you understand the important information.

Underlining or highlighting information is one way to help you remember important ideas in a source text. It can be done in different ways. Usually, students develop their own style. These are some suggestions.

When you underline or highlight:

- Look for the main ideas and important points.
- Identify key words and phrases.
- Identify details that give an example or explanation.
- Identify quotes and figures you may need to refer to later.
- Choose entire sentences or sections of text if it helps you connect and remember ideas.

Taking notes is another way to help you remember important ideas and key terms in source materials.

When you take notes:

- Use the margins or empty spaces on the page for your notes.
- Write only important words and phrases (complete sentences are not necessary).
- Write the main ideas in your own words.
- Add your own ideas, reactions, or questions.

Later, your notes, and any information you have underlined or highlighted, will help you think about the topic, prepare for exams, or write an essay.

Notes:

- Underlining and notetaking are useful skills for test taking, especially when you need to read or listen to a passage and then answer questions or write about it.
- Professors and universities often post their lectures online. Students can download lecture transcripts (what the professor said during the lecture) for study and review. This is a great way to get information that you may have missed from the lecture. On the printed transcript, you can underline and take notes and look up vocabulary you do not know. This gives you more time to explore and understand the ideas.

A. *Read this lecture transcript from a psychology class. Notice the phrases a student underlined in the first section of the lecture.*

Modern Psychology—Spring Term
Lecture: Wednesday, May 10

Professor: Today, I'm going to talk about <u>new research that looks at personality traits and dishonesty</u>.

First, why might researchers be interested in this? Do you think <u>people are being more dishonest than in the past</u>? Certainly, in schools, studies show that academic cheating is up 50 percent. In the news, we see top athletes going to jail for taking performance-enhancing drugs;[1] corporate executives cheating customers and employees; people we admire for their strong ethics[2] displaying the most scandalous[3] behavior. Regardless of whether dishonesty is on the rise, being trustworthy[4] affects how well societies prosper. Thus, if <u>researchers can tell us if one type of person is more likely to cheat than another</u>, maybe this information <u>can help us prevent dishonesty</u>.

<u>Recent studies</u> have shed some light on[5] <u>two distinct cheating types—brazen[6] cheaters and rationalizing cheaters</u>. Let's look at the <u>brazen type</u> first. This type of <u>cheater cheats openly or on purpose</u>. For example, a student copies answers and keeps them hidden, so he or she can look at them during a test.

The <u>other type</u> of cheater <u>rationalizes or justifies his or her behavior</u>. This type <u>finds a reason to make his or her cheating acceptable</u>. An example of this would be the student who copies and pastes text from the Internet for a paper. This rationalizing type thinks, "Everyone else is doing it, so it must OK. The text is available. Why shouldn't I copy it?"

Before I go further, let me ask you a question. What does all of this information suggest?

---

[1]*performance-enhancing drugs*—drugs that people sometimes use illegally to improve their sports performance
[2]*ethics*—moral rules or principles of behavior for deciding what is right and wrong
[3]*scandalous*—completely immoral and shocking
[4]*trustworthy*—able to be trusted or depended on
[5]*shed some light on*—to make something easier to understand
[6]*brazen*—showing that you do not feel ashamed about behavior that most people think is wrong or immoral

B. *Work with another student. Discuss these questions:*

- What information is underlined? Why?

- Did the student underline only words and phrases or complete sentences?

- Would you underline additional words, phrases, or sentences? If so, which ones? Why? If not, why not?

A. *Read the next part of the lecture transcript. Notice the student's notes in the margins.*

Professor: Before I go further, let me ask you a question. What does all of this information suggest?

Can we justify dishonesty in some situations? (starving person stealing food) – not cheating in school

Student One: That it's very easy for some people to justify cheating.

focus on importance of trust, honesty

Professor: OK. Any ideas how we can change this behavior in school and the workplace?

Student Two: Maybe have some classes to teach ethical behavior?

Should not be just for business students—could be for students/ company employees

Professor: Yes. In fact, some business schools are now requiring students to take business ethics courses.

Student Three: I think there need to be stronger punishments or clearly stated rules about behavior. Maybe rewards?

Student Four: My school had peer mentors—classmates who helped other classmates. Peer mentors could help classmates who were having trouble.

* Good idea—could it work for companies, too?

Professor: All good ideas. Just what the researchers suggested . . .

B. *Read the whole lecture again. Add your own notes and questions. Remember: Keep your notes brief. Do not write complete sentences.*

C. *Compare notes with another student. What is the same? What is different?*

Further Practice

Journal or Blog Topic *(See Part 1, Units 1 and 2.)*

• Imagine you are a student in the class from the lecture in Exercises 5 and 6. Write a response to the professor, giving your opinion and ideas about the issue.

Study Questions

Textbooks and handouts from your teacher often include study questions that help you understand and analyze a topic. Taking the time to answer these questions will help you check your understanding of the subject.

If there are no study questions included with a reading assignment, you can create your own by asking yourself questions beginning with *Wh-*, for example, *Who, What, Where, When,* and *Why.* In addition the word *How* is also usually included in this set, although it does not begin with *Wh-.* These are called information questions.

EXERCISE 7

A. *Read the study questions. Underline the* **Wh-** *words. Then read the article in Exercise 4 on pages 136–137 again and write your answers.*

Study Questions

1. Where did the study take place? _____

2. What are some traits of students who are less likely to cheat?

   _____

3. What opinion do the students who are more likely to cheat have of other students?

   _____

4. According to the study, which group of students is more likely to rationalize cheating, the one that scored higher or the one that scored lower?

   _____

5. Who are the "academic heroes?" _____

6. According to the researchers, why are the students who scored in the 29 percent

   range so important? _____

B. *On a separate piece of paper, write three* **Wh-** *study questions based on the lecture transcript in Exercise 5.*

C. *Exchange papers with another student. Write your answers to your partner's questions. Then check your answers together. Were they correct?*

First-Response Journals

As you know, a journal is a place to write down your thoughts, ideas, and feelings. First-response journals are a way to start making connections between source materials and your own knowledge and experiences. Your response journal will help you review exam materials and form opinions for writing assignments.

Your journal may be shared with your classmates and teacher, or it may just be private.

Guidelines for Writing a First-Response Journal

- Write down any ideas and thoughts that come to your mind about the topic. Don't worry about whether you think they are good ideas or not.

- Use the personal pronoun *I* to express opinions, feelings, and questions about the topic. You can use phrases such as:

    I think . . .
    I feel . . .
    I believe . . .
    I wonder . . .
    I don't know whether . . .

- Include examples or brief stories from your own life and experience that connect to the topic.

- Don't worry about grammar or spelling mistakes.

Note: After you write your first-response journal, you can use it to review or study. Go back and read what you wrote. Highlight important words, phrases, or sentences, and take notes on any questions you still have about the topic.

WRITING TASK

Write a first-response journal entry about one of the topics in this unit.

A. *Read this sample passage from a first-response journal.*

> In some situations, I think maybe we can justify dishonesty;
> for example, if it is a matter of life or death, like if a person
> is starving, and they steal something to eat.
>
> I know cheating in school is wrong. Sometimes I see other
> students in my classes cheating. I don't think it's my place to
> say anything to them.
>
> I like the ideas in the lecture about ethics classes and peer
> mentors. I think it might help prevent cheating—at least it
> would make some students think twice before they cheat. If we
> had a discussion at the beginning of the term, students could
> talk about honesty and trust, and how cheating is not fair for
> the students who don't cheat . . .

B. *Think about the topics of the readings in this unit. What connections can you make to your own experiences and knowledge?*

Some examples may include . . .
- someone you know who cheated in school, or different ways students cheat in school
- a story you read, a movie you saw, or a personal story about the issue of honesty/dishonesty
- something you know about Internet file sharing
- an honest person you know

C. *In your journal, or on a separate piece of paper, write a first-response journal entry about the lecture or article in this unit. Write for at least 15 minutes. Follow the guidelines on page 142.*

D. *Discuss the opinions and ideas you wrote about with the class.*

Prewriting Techniques

Prewriting, or brainstorming, is usually the starting point for gathering ideas about a topic you will write about. The prewriting stage is a time to let your ideas flow without having to worry about organization or grammar. It also shows you whether you have enough information about your topic, or if you need to do more research.

The prewriting techniques introduced in this unit can also be useful if you experience writer's block—times when you have trouble thinking of what to write.

There are a number of prewriting techniques. In this unit, you will practice the following:

- Freewriting
- Listing
- Clustering
- Journalist Questions
- Group Discussion—Problem Solving

Warm Up

A. *How do you usually gather or organize your ideas for writing assignments (in English or in your first language)? Check (✓) the statements that are true for you. Add any other activities you do that are not listed.*

I think silently about the topic and the assignment.	
I write a lot of ideas and notes.	
I start writing the assignment immediately.	
I do research online and read books about the topic.	
I try to find examples of similar writing about the topic.	
I talk about my ideas with my teacher or with a classmate.	

B. *Compare answers with another student. Which activities have been most helpful in preparing you for writing assignments?*

FREEWRITING

When you **freewrite,** you begin writing, and you continue writing as much as you can without stopping, usually for several minutes. You do NOT stop to correct grammar mistakes or rewrite sentences.

There are different types of freewriting. You have probably already done some freewriting activities in this book.

In this unit, you will practice **freestyle freewriting.** Freestyle freewriting is a warm-up for your brain and fingers—just to get you started writing. You simply write down any thought that comes into your head even if the thought is "I can't think of anything to write." Eventually, another thought will come, and you write it down. The point is to keep writing.

You can practice freestyle freewriting with a pen and paper or on your computer. If you choose to use a computer, turn off the monitor (screen) and just type. This will help you focus on your thoughts and ideas instead of the grammar or spelling mistakes on the screen.

> *Look at the sample of a student's freestyle freewrite, completed with the computer screen turned off. Notice that the freewriting contains mistakes.*

I don't know what to write. I don't know what to write and I have to keep write with my screen turned off. I hope something comes into my head. Iam not a very good typist. How about Iwrite about the weather or the green leaves that I can see outside my window? I just remembered a classmate who said she did wrote with her computer screen off. She said she typed while looking out her window. Who was it? I hate it when i cant think of someone's name. This is so new to me, but I like looking out my window or even at something other than my computor screen. Oh, I didn't realize I have started writing and words are coming out thru my fingers! I see people walking their dogs. I saw a really good show on television last night. I can't remember the title but it was about building a castle hundreds of years ago in ENgland. It is so quiet in my room right now . . .

For this exercise, choose Exercise A, Pen and Paper Freewrite, *or Exercise B,* Computer Freewrite.

Remember

When you freewrite, do not worry about grammar or vocabulary. If you cannot think of a word, it is OK to use your first language. Just keep writing.

A. *Pen and Paper Freewrite: On a clean piece of paper, freewrite for five minutes. Write anything that comes to your mind. Do not stop writing.*

B. *Computer Freewrite: Turn off your computer screen. If you have a laptop, lower the screen, so you cannot see it. Type anything that comes to your mind for five minutes. After five minutes, stop and print out your freewrite.*

Note: This exercise can be done in class, at home, or in a computer lab.

C. *Work with another student. Discuss these questions:*

- Which style of freewrite (pen and paper or computer) did you choose? Why? In the future, will you choose the same style?

- Was it difficult to start your freestyle freewrite? Why or why not?

- How did you feel when you first started? As you continued to write?

- Do you think freestyle freewriting might be helpful for your writing in English? Why or why not?

LISTING

Lists are simple, helpful tools for gathering and sorting ideas. Making a list of your ideas about a topic is another prewriting brainstorming technique. **Listing** is especially useful when you have chosen a topic and need to gather ideas for what to say about it.

For example, for a report on private and public universities, you might brainstorm a list of advantages and disadvantages of attending each type of university.

A. **Work in a group. For five minutes, brainstorm as many ideas as you can about the advantages and disadvantages of private and public schools. Choose one student to list the group's ideas.**

Remember

When you brainstorm, the point is to list as many ideas as you can. Work quickly and list all your ideas. Do not stop to think about or choose the ones you like the best. You can do that after you complete the brainstorm.

B. **Join another group. Look at your list of advantages and disadvantages of private and public schools. Complete the chart.**

Public Schools
Choose two advantages both groups listed.
–
–
Choose two disadvantages both groups listed.
–
–
Private Schools
Choose two advantages both groups listed.
–
–
Choose two disadvantages both groups listed.
–
–
Which ideas could you use to write a short paragraph?
Which type of school would you choose? Why?

C. **Share your answers with the class.**

A. *Try your own listing brainstorm. On a separate piece of paper, make a list of one of these topics:*

- Interesting uses for a toothbrush
- Ways to stay organized
- Things to do on a rainy Saturday

- World's most dangerous pets
- Best ways to save money
- Top 10 dance songs

B. *Share your list with a partner. Add any new ideas to your lists. Save your brainstorm to use later in this unit.*

Note: Listing is a good strategy for quickly gathering ideas for a topic on a timed essay test. (See Part 3, Unit 9.)

CLUSTERING

Clustering is another way to brainstorm ideas. A cluster is the same as a word web or an idea web.

You start by writing the topic in the center of your paper and circling it. Then, you write down all the ideas you can think of around the topic and circle them, too. As you think of more ideas, you circle them and connect them to the other circles with a line. When you finish, your paper will have a series of connected circles with different ideas about the topic.

Example:

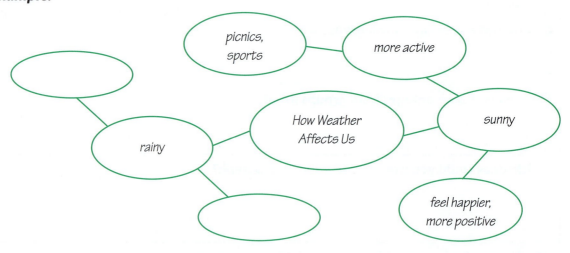

A. **Look at the example cluster on page 148. Discuss these questions with the class:**

- What is the main topic? Where is it written?

- How does the cluster represent the person's thoughts? In what order do you think the circles were written?

B. **On your own, add your ideas to the blank circles in the example. Continue adding more circles and ideas to the cluster. Then share your ideas with another student.**

A. **Work with another student. Choose one of these topics to brainstorm about:**

- Qualities of a good student, coach, athlete, or boss
- Hiking
- Safety in the workplace
- Recycling
- Saving money
- Reality TV shows

B. **On your own, make a cluster about the topic on a separate piece of paper.**

C. **Compare your clusters. How are they the same? How are they different? Does your cluster contain enough information for you to write a paragraph or more about your topic?**

JOURNALIST QUESTIONS

Journalist questions are information questions, beginning with *Wh-*: *Who, What, Where, When, Why,* and *How.* Journalists use these questions to help organize their news stories.

In prewriting, asking and answering these kinds of questions will help you find out what you already know and what you still need to find out about a topic.

Example:

Topic: *The history of basketball*

Journalist questions: *Who invented the sport? What were the original rules? When was it invented? Where was the first professional game? Why is it so popular in the U.S.? How much money do professional players make?*

Work with another student. Read the topic and the journalist questions and answers. Add more ideas under each question. Add more questions and answers.

Topic: "Materialistic Kids: The New Consumers"

What is "materialistic"?

- Longman Dictionary of American English: *the belief that money and possessions are more important than art, religion, morality, etc.*

What is a "consumer"?

- _____

What do kids want to buy?

- video games
- jewelry
- _____
- _____

Where are kids buying things?

- malls
- _____
- _____

How do they find out about products to buy?

- advertisements
- _____
- _____

Where do they see advertisements?

- on TV
- _____
- _____

Why do they want to buy new things?

- want to feel stylish or beautiful
- _____
- _____

How does having or wanting too many things affect kids?

- kids unhappy/angry when they can't get what they want

- _____

- _____

> **Note:** For another example of journalist questions for paragraphs, see Unit 4.

EXERCISE 7

A. *Choose one of these topics. Complete the chart with journalist (Wh-) questions about the topic.*

- Tablet computer technology
- What is a planet?
- Effective business strategies
- Crimes on university campuses
- New car technology

***Who* Questions**
***What* Questions**
***When* Questions**
***Where* Questions**
***Why* Questions**
***How* Questions**

B. *Compare journalist questions with another student. Try to answer the questions together. Write your answers. What do you still need to know?*

GROUP DISCUSSION—PROBLEM SOLVING

Students, business people, parents, and politicians face problems every day. These problems can be simple or complicated. Being able to problem-solve is a valuable skill. It often involves identifying and understanding a problem and then making decisions about how to solve the problem. For difficult problems, a group discussion can be an effective way to brainstorm solutions. This method of prewriting is particularly useful for developing ideas for problem/solution paragraphs and essays.

EXERCISE 8

Work with another student. Read the writer's notes from a group discussion about how to prevent plagiarism. Discuss these questions:

- What is the problem?
- What people or organizations did the group consider as part of the solution?
- What solutions do you think will be the most effective? Why?

Plagiarism Prevention—Group Discussion Notes

School
- make online information available for all students about what plagiarism is
- establish clear policies and consequences for plagiarizing

Teachers
- enforce school policies
- teach students how to refer to sources and ideas that are not their own
- focus on why writing in their own words is important

Students
- some students come from cultures that do not have clear rules about what plagiarism is/need to understand how "cutting and pasting" can get them into trouble
- understand that it is considered cheating and may affect them later in work situations
- sign a contract promising not to plagiarize

A. *Work in a group. Have a group discussion to brainstorm possible solutions to the problem below. Take notes on your discussion.*

Problem: Many students do not read the newspaper or follow local or international news. How can this be changed?

B. *Discuss these questions with your group:*
- How many solutions did you find?
- Which solutions do you think will be the most effective? Why?
- What other information do you need to find a solution to the problem?

Further Practice

Journal or Blog Topics *(See Part 1, Units 1 and 2.)*
- Choose one of these problems:
  - Many young people today have unhealthy diets and do not get enough exercise.
  - Around the world, there are many people who cannot afford basic healthcare for their families.
  - Overcrowding is a problem in many places; however, the world population is over 7 billion and growing.
- Use one of the brainstorming techniques from this unit (freewriting, listing, clusters, journalist questions, group discussion) to brainstorm ideas for how to solve the problem. Then write your ideas in your journal or on your class blog.

WRITING TASK

Complete a prewriting brainstorm and use it to write a composition.

A. *Choose one of the topics from this unit. Go back and read your prewriting brainstorm about the topic:*
- Exercise 2: List—public schools vs. private schools
- Exercise 5: Cluster—topic of choice
- Exercise 7: Journalist questions—topic of choice
- Exercise 9: Group discussion—students and the news

B. *Freewrite for five minutes about the topic.*

C. *Look at your information about the topic. Do you have enough to write a composition about it? What else do you want/need to know?*

D. *Use your freewrite and your prewriting brainstorm to write a short composition (two or three paragraphs) about the topic. Remember to include the characteristics of good academic paragraphs. (See Unit 2.)*

Check Your Writing

A. *Use this form to check your own composition, or exchange compositions with another student and check each other's writing.*

Composition Checklist

The composition . . .

1. is the correct length. ☐

2. is about one of the topics from this unit. ☐

3. follows the guidelines for good academic paragraphs. ☐

4. Are there any sentences you don't understand? If so, write a question mark (?) in front of them on the composition.

5. What changes do you suggest to improve the composition?

_____

_____

_____

_____

_____

_____

B. *Make changes to improve your composition. Remember to check your writing for grammar, spelling, and punctuation errors.*

UNIT 6 Thesis Statements, Introductions, and Conclusions

This unit focuses on three key elements of an academic essay. A clear thesis statement, a well-organized introduction, and a strong, clear conclusion are essential for expressing your main idea and communicating the overall aim or focus of your academic essay.

Warm Up

A. *Work in a group. Look at the photos and discuss these questions:*

- What is happening in each photo?
- What do you think about what is happening in the photo?

B. *On your own, choose a photo and write a sentence to capture your opinion of it. Then share your sentence with your group.*

THESIS STATEMENTS

Academic writing focuses on one topic and one main idea about the topic. A **thesis statement** is a statement of the writer's main idea or opinion about the topic. In this way, a thesis statement is like a topic sentence in a paragraph. (See Unit 2, page 102.)

The thesis statement is usually found in the introduction of an essay. Taking time to develop a clear thesis statement will help you determine what you really want to say in your essay.

Thesis statements must be broad enough to cover the entire main idea; that is, all the information, opinions, and ideas expressed by the writer in the essay.

Look at the two examples of thesis statements. Which one do you think is more effective? Read the explanations and compare your ideas.

Statement 1

Students in graduate business programs are cheating more than any other students.

Statement 2

Graduate business programs can deter students from cheating with prevention plans that include ethics courses, clear punishments, and support from teachers and classmates.

Explanation

Statement 1 is a fact. It does not express a purpose or main idea. Therefore, it is not an effective thesis statement.

However, statement 2 expresses:

1. the intention of the essay:

Graduate business programs can deter students from cheating . . .

and

2. how the main idea will be developed in the essay:

. . . plans that include ethics courses, clear punishments, and support from teachers and classmates.

From this thesis statement it is clear to the reader that the writer will present the subtopics *ethics courses, clear punishments, and support from teachers and classmates* in the body paragraphs of the essay.

Look at two more examples of thesis statements.

Statement 3

Many people do not know which career path to choose.

Statement 4

People can get help choosing a career path by talking to friends and family, taking personality tests, and doing an internship.

Explanation

Like statement 1 in the previous examples, statement 3 is a fact and does not express a purpose or main idea. It is not an effective thesis statement.

However, statement 4 expresses:

1. the intention of the essay:

People can get help choosing a career path . . .

and

2. how the main idea will be developed in the essay:

. . . by talking to friends and family, taking personality tests, and doing an internship.

It is clear to the reader that the writer will present the subtopics *talking to family and friends,* *taking personality tests,* and *doing an internship* in the body paragraphs of the essay.

In this way, a thesis statement shows your plan for your essay. You can think of a thesis statement as an umbrella. The handle is the main idea, and the top is broad, so it covers the topic, and each section is a subtopic that fills out or supports the topic.

Thesis Statement:
(covers the main idea <u>and</u> how it will be developed)

Graduate business programs can deter students from cheating with prevention plans that include ethics courses, clear punishments, and support from teachers and classmates.

How the Main Idea Will Be Developed

Subtopic 1	**Subtopic 2**	**Subtopic 3**
ethics courses	*clear punishments*	*support from teachers and classmates*

Main Idea:
Prevention plans can deter students from cheating.

A. *Read the statements. Decide whether each one is a fact or a main idea that can be developed in an essay. Check (✓) the statements that are main ideas.*

1. Sweden does not permit advertising on television to children younger than 12 years old.	
2. Athletics can teach students important life skills such as team building, health and nutrition, and responsibility.	
3. College costs are skyrocketing, but students can lower tuition bills by working part-time, searching for scholarships, or looking into low-interest loan options.	
4. Without empathy, we will lose our ability to build a strong community and understand others.	
5. Plumpy Nut is a low-cost, peanut-butter paste with vitamins and minerals.	
6. A recent report shows that 21 percent of college students have credit card debt of $3,000 or more.	
7. English is the official language of the International Olympic Committee.	
8. Learning how to control negative emotions can improve relationships with family members, friends, and coworkers.	
9. Japan and the United States competed for the Women's World Cup Soccer title in Germany in 2011.	
10. Finding the time to relax and rejuvenate will be good for both your mind and your body.	

B. *Compare answers with another student. Answer these questions about the statements you marked with a check (✓).*

1. What is the main idea?
2. Which points will the writer develop in the essay?

Example:

Thesis statement: *Athletics can teach students important life skills such as team building, health and nutrition, and responsibility.*

Main idea: *Athletics can teach students important life skills.*

Points the writer will develop: *team building, health and nutrition, and responsibility*

TOPICS AND FOCUS

Big topics, like psychology, sports, and business, are too broad (general) to cover in an essay. As you think about your topic, you will have to narrow your focus to make it clearer. Look at the topics below and notice how the writer narrowed them down into focused ideas.

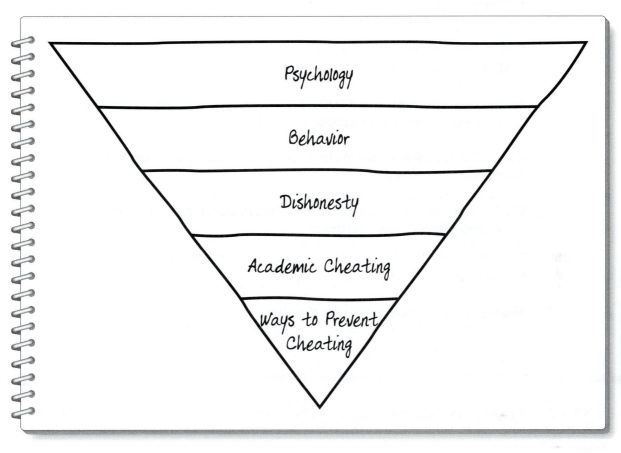

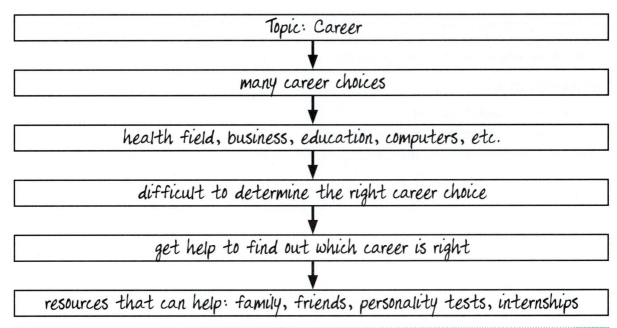

A. *Choose one of these topics. What do you know about the topic? To get ideas about the topic, do a prewriting brainstorm (freewrite, list, cluster, etc.). (See Unit 5.)*

- Honesty and sports
- Stress and academics
- How advertisements influence children
- Money and happiness

B. *Narrow down the topic into a focused main idea you can write about. Draw a diagram like the ones on page 159.*

C. *Write a thesis statement for the topic. Make sure it covers the main idea you developed in Exercise B.*

D. *Work in a group. Take turns reading your thesis statements aloud. For each statement, discuss these questions:*

- What is the main idea? Is it broad enough to cover the information about the topic?
- Which points will the writer develop in the essay?

E. *Share your thesis statements with the class.*

INTRODUCTIONS

Good beginnings are important, whether it is meeting someone for the first time, making a phone call, or composing an academic essay. Each of these beginnings follows an expected format. In an essay, it is the introduction.

The **introduction** begins with general information about the topic and then moves to the specific focus or purpose of the essay—the thesis. The last sentence in the introduction is usually the thesis statement. Introductory paragraphs are usually shorter than body paragraphs.

Introductions should . . .

- capture the reader's interest.
- present general information about the topic.
- include a thesis statement that gives the writer's intent.

Read the sample introduction. Then discuss the questions with the class.

Introduction

In a recent study, up to 25 percent of students said they had used stimulants called "cognitive enhancers" to help them study and achieve better grades. Cognitive enhancers are stimulants—a type of drug that causes the brain to feel more awake or active. Many students feel pressure to get good grades in order to get jobs or be accepted into graduate programs. However, students do not realize the dangerous side effects these drugs produce, including disrupted sleep, moodiness, and loss of appetite. Students need to know they can lower their stress and succeed academically by making a study plan and eating right.

- What is the topic?
- Where is the thesis statement in the paragraph?
- What is the main idea? Which points will the writer develop in the essay?
- What other information is included in the introduction?

Hooks

Any good movie, book, or article grabs the interest of the audience from the start. In a movie, there may be an action sequence or stimulating dialogue to draw you into the story. In writing, there are several techniques, called "hooks," that writers use to capture their readers from the start. The hook is usually the first sentence, or one of the first few sentences, of the introduction.

Some types of hooks include . . .

an anecdote a short story or narration that illustrates or exemplifies the main point

Jenny sat down with her computer to look through the various job postings once again. There was a notice for a sales representative and another one for a computer technician. She knew she liked talking to people, but she also liked problem-solving. She did not know which position would be the best fit for her. She felt frustrated and lost. She wished she knew what to do.

a surprising fact or statistic *Seventy-seven percent of the students surveyed said they had cheated.*

a famous quote or saying *"That man is the richest whose pleasures are the cheapest."—Henry David Thoreau*

a question *What is the leading cause of stress among university students?*

A. **Look at the sample introductions. Identify the type of hook used in each one. More than one type of hook may be used.**

> anecdote   surprising fact or statistic   famous quote or saying   question

1. Type of hook: _____

In a recent study, up to 25 percent of students said they had used stimulants called "cognitive enhancers" to help them study and achieve better grades. Cognitive enhancers are stimulants—drugs that cause the brain to feel more awake or active. Many students feel pressure to get good grades in order to get jobs or be accepted into graduate programs. However, students do not realize the dangerous side effects these drugs produce, including disrupted sleep, moodiness, and loss of appetite. Students need to know they can lower their stress and succeed academically by making a study plan and eating right.

2. Type of hook: _____

My life changed dramatically when I met my wife. At first, I did not notice her. She didn't have a strong personality and she was not outspoken. She was just another one of my coworkers when I worked in a public relations firm. However, after we worked together on a group project, developing a marketing plan for a client, I gradually got to know her and we became friends. Over time, I began to realize that she was a special person and we fell in love. We have been married for two years now. Being friends before marrying can lead to a successful marriage because it gives you time to build a strong bond and form an understanding of each other.

3. Type of hook: _____

Do you remember the classmate who never studied? The one who spent her free time with the troublemakers? That was me until one of my teachers, who was also the volleyball coach, insisted that I try out for the team. Playing volleyball changed my life. It gave me the opportunity to become physically fit, learn about being responsible, and develop useful life skills.

B. **On a separate piece of paper, rewrite the start of each introduction from Part A, using a different type of hook. Share your new hooks with the class.**

A. *Use the thesis statement you wrote in Exercise 2 to write an introductory paragraph. Remember to add a hook.*

B. *When you finish writing, check your introduction for the following:*

☐ The topic is narrowed down into a focused main idea.

☐ The paragraph includes a hook.

☐ The thesis statement is broad enough to cover the main idea.

☐ The intent or plan for your essay is clear.

C. *Share your introduction with another student. Look again at the checklist in Exercise B and discuss any missing parts.*

CONCLUSIONS

A **concluding paragraph** is similar to an introductory paragraph. It is shorter than the body paragraphs and restates (repeats) the thesis statement and the important points from the essay. However, it does not repeat the exact words from the introduction; it uses different words to express the same idea.

A concluding paragraph does not introduce new information. Often, the writer makes a final recommendation, warning, or suggestion to leave the reader with a definite idea or impression about the topic.

There are certain transitions or signal words that indicate the conclusion of an essay.

In conclusion, . . .	*Finally, . . .*
To conclude . . .	*To sum up, . . .*
All in all, . . .	*In closing . . .*

Read the sample introduction. Then read the two conclusions on the next page. Which conclusion do you think best matches the introduction? Discuss your ideas with the class.

Introduction

In a recent study, up to 25 percent of students said they had used stimulants called "cognitive enhancers" to help them study and achieve better grades. Cognitive enhancers are stimulants—drugs that cause the brain to feel more awake or active. Many students feel pressure to get good grades in order to get jobs or be accepted into graduate programs. However, students do not realize the dangerous side effects these drugs produce, including disrupted sleep, moodiness, and loss of appetite. Students need to know they can lower their stress and succeed academically by making a study plan and eating right.

(continued)

Conclusion 1

On college campuses across the country students will have to decide if they need the help of stimulants to help them cope with the stress caused by competition for grades and jobs. In addition, some students feel stress because of the high cost of tuition. Students need to know they can lower their stress and succeed academically by making a study plan and eating right.

Conclusion 2

In conclusion, today's college students face enormous pressure to do well in school. Many of them feel they cannot compete without study drugs. However, students can reduce stress and raise their overall grades without stimulants if they change their study routines and follow a healthy diet. If students do not learn how to reach their goals without the aid of cognitive enhancers, they may suffer serious, long-lasting consequences.

EXERCISE 7

A. *Write a concluding paragraph based on your introductory paragraph from Exercise 5.*

B. *When you finish writing, check your conclusion for the following:*

☐ The paragraph uses a transition or signal word.

☐ The paragraph restates the thesis and main idea.

☐ The paragraph uses words that are different from those used in the introduction.

☐ The paragraph includes a final comment such as a recommendation, a warning, or an opinion.

C. *Share your concluding paragraph with another student. Look again at the checklist in Exercise B and discuss any missing parts.*

WRITING TASK

Write an effective introduction and a matching concluding paragraph.

A. *Choose a different topic from Exercise 2—one you did NOT use to write a thesis statement.*

B. *On a separate piece of paper, do a prewriting brainstorm (freewrite, list, cluster, etc.) about the topic.*

C. *On a new piece of paper, use your brainstorm to write an effective thesis statement. Then use your thesis statement to write an introduction. Include one of the types of hooks introduced in this unit.*

D. *Read your introduction and make changes to improve it.*

E. *Write a conclusion to match your introduction. Use an appropriate transition or signal word.*

Check Your Writing

A. *Use this form to check your own writing, or exchange paragraphs with another student and check each other's writing.*

Introduction and Conclusion Checklist

The introduction . . .

1. includes a hook. ☐

2. includes a thesis statement that is broad enough to cover the main idea. ☐

3. makes clear the intent or plan for the essay. ☐

4. What changes do you suggest to improve the paragraph?

_____

_____

_____

_____

The conclusion . . .

5. uses an appropriate transition or signal word. ☐

6. restates the thesis and main idea. ☐

7. uses words that are different from those used in the introduction. ☐

8. includes a final comment such as a recommendation, a warning, or an opinion. ☐

9. What changes do you suggest to improve the paragraph?

_____

_____

_____

_____

_____

B. *Make changes to improve your paragraphs. Remember to check your writing for grammar, spelling, and punctuation errors.*

Organizing and Drafting

At this stage of the writing process, you have already developed your main idea, brainstormed details, and researched supporting facts and information. Now you are ready to organize your essay.

The way you organize your essay depends on what you are trying to say. For example, if you are writing a biography, you may use chronological sequence. If you are writing about a political movement, you may use a cause/effect pattern. If you are presenting a proposal, you may use problem/solution organization. You may need to use one or more of these organizing patterns in your essays. (See more on patterns of organization in Unit 2.)

Good writers use different strategies to organize their information. In this unit, you will focus on using these strategies for two common types of academic essays: the Cause/Effect Essay and the Problem/Solution Essay.

Warm Up

Work in a group. Discuss these questions:

- Do you think it's important to be organized?
- Do you think you are an organized person? Why or why not?
- What kinds of things do you organize?
- What helps you stay organized? What makes it difficult to be organized?

CAUSE/EFFECT ORGANIZATION

A **cause/effect** essay lists and explains causes (why something happened) and effects (results or consequences of something).

There are different patterns possible in a cause-effect essay.

Examples:

Pattern 1: Several *causes* for one *effect*:

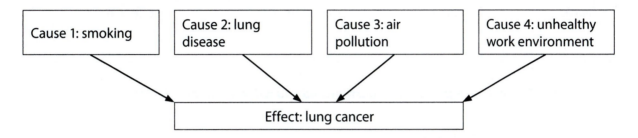

Pattern 2: Several *effects* from one *cause*:

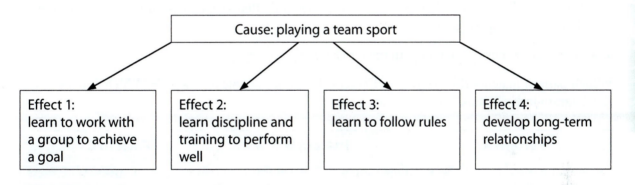

EXERCISE 1

    A. *Work with another student. Complete the diagram with reasons why people decide to own pets. Add more causes if you can:*

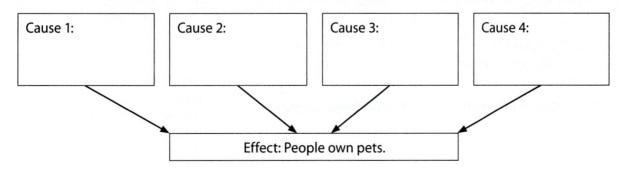

    B. *Compare diagrams with a partner. Did you write the same causes?*

A. *Work with another student. Complete the diagram with the effects of cramming (waiting until the last minute to study) for an exam. Add more effects if you can.*

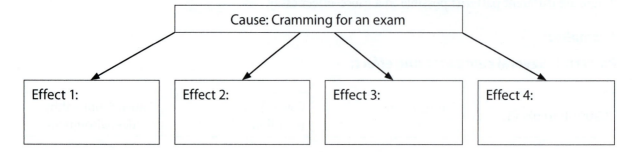

B. *Compare diagrams with a partner. Did you write the same effects?*

Cause/Effect Essay Patterns

Within both patterns in Exercises 1 and 2, it is important to note that the causes and effects are closely related. Writers may choose to focus on causes and effects separately, or to alternate causes and effects within a paragraph or essay.

The chart below shows different patterns for cause/effect essays.

Which pattern matches the diagram in Exercise 1 (reasons people own a pet)? Which one matches the diagram in Exercise 2 (effects of cramming)?

Pattern A	**Pattern B**	**Pattern C**
Several Causes → One Effect	**One Cause → Several Effects**	**Alternating Causes and Effects**
Introductory Paragraph – Introduces the effect and gives some examples of causes **Body Paragraph 1** – Introduces and explains cause 1 **Body Paragraph 2** – Introduces and explains cause 2 **Concluding Paragraph**	**Introductory Paragraph** – Introduces the cause and gives some examples of effects **Body Paragraph 1** – Introduces and explains effect 1 **Body Paragraph 2** – Introduces and explains effect 2 **Concluding Paragraph**	**Introductory Paragraph** – Introduces the causes and effects **Body Paragraph 1** *Sub-topic A* – Introduces cause 1 – Explains effect 1 – Introduces cause 2 – Explains effect 2 **Body Paragraph 2** *Sub-topic B* – Introduces cause 1 – Explains effect 1 – Introduces cause 2 – Explains effect 2 **Concluding Paragraph**

Preparing to Write: Sorting Causes and Effects

Sorting the information you have gathered about a topic before you start writing is a good strategy for organizing your ideas.

Graphic organizers, like clusters (see Unit 5) and charts, are particularly useful for sorting information.

There are many different types of graphic organizers. In this unit, you will practice using two-column charts to prepare to write cause/effect and problem/solution essays.

EXERCISE 3

A. *Read a student's brainstorm for a cause/effect essay titled "How Companies Gain Trust."*

Gaining Employee Trust

Companies make honesty responsibility of employees

Expense accounts—companies let employees decide how much to spend

Employees feel trusted, responsible for lower spending

Companies treat employees like honest workers

Employees feel trusted, so they work harder

Employees don't feel watched, so they want to invest more in company's success

Gaining Customer Trust

Companies should have policies that protect the customer

Companies should make it easy for customers to return items

Customers will buy more in the long run

Companies should make sure products are safe and high quality

Bad products result in lost money and customers

B. *Work with another student. Decide which items on the student's list on page 169 are causes and which are effects. Write them in the correct columns in the chart*

Gaining Employee Trust		Gaining Customer Trust	
Causes	**Effects**	**Causes**	**Effects**

EXERCISE 4

A. *Read the student's essay. Notice the bold transitions for the cause/effect pattern.*

Sanjay Patel

Business Ethics

Professor Wyatt

December 10, 2012

How Companies Gain Trust

Can we really trust big business? Most people say no, but a growing number of companies are reconsidering the importance of trust. Building trust takes time and effort on the company's part. Some companies today are trying new approaches, in addition to traditional ones, to gain the trust of both employees and customers.

One thing that seems to make a difference is whether or not a company shows that it trusts its employees. For example, many companies have strict policies about employees' travel and entertainment spending. These policies are created to protect the company from employees' overspending or cheating the company. Now, instead of managing every penny, companies allow employees to decide how much to spend on business-related meals, hotels, and airfare. **As a result,** employees feel responsible for finding lower prices and saving the company money. Companies that treat their employees like honest workers are getting a stronger workforce in return. Workers do not feel as if they are always being watched; **consequently,** they become more invested in their company's success.

Although honesty between employee and employer is important, developing customers' trust is essential. Without customers, there is no company. To gain customers' trust, a company has to focus on ways to build a good relationship. One way to do this is for a company to establish strong policies that protect its customers. An example is a company's return policy. Customers should receive full refunds with or without receipts for any item they return—used or unused. **If** customers feel they can shop without worrying about returning unwanted items, they will buy more. Another policy, and perhaps the most important trust factor for customers, is product safety. More than once, newspaper headlines have alerted customers to dangers such as lead paint in children's toys or malfunctioning car parts long before the manufacturer came forward and took action. For the companies, these unsafe products **resulted in** not only losing millions of dollars, but also losing their customers for life.

Finally, trustworthiness is the foundation for successful business because it **affects** everyone. New ideas along with established policies are helping companies achieve this goal. Companies that are not rethinking the importance of trust may be out of business sooner rather than later.

B. *Work with another student. Discuss these questions. Write your answers.*

1. Does the organization follow Pattern A, Pattern B, or Pattern C in the chart on page 168? _____

2. According to the essay, what are some reasons (causes) businesses are working to gain employee and customer trust? _____
What are some of the effects for these businesses? _____

3. How many paragraphs are in the essay? _____

4. Which paragraphs are shorter? Why? _____

5. Which paragraphs are longer? Why? _____

(continued)

6. What kind of hook is used in the introduction? (See Unit 6.) _____

7. What is the thesis statement? Where is it located in the introduction? (See Unit 6.)

   _____

8. What supporting details are given in the essay? _____

   _____

   _____

9. Underline the restated thesis statement in the conclusion. How is it different from the thesis statement in the introduction? (See Unit 6.) _____

10. What kind of final comment (warning, suggestion, recommendation, question) does the writer give in the conclusion? _____

PROBLEM/SOLUTION ORGANIZATION

A problem/solution essay pattern has two parts: the problem section and the solution section.

A problem/solution essay identifies a problem and why it is important to fix it. Then it proposes a solution to the problem.

Problem Section	Solution Section

Identifies the problem
Example:
 – *city has ugly, dirty public areas*
 – *people have no place to sit, enjoy the outdoors*
 	
Explains why the problem should be fixed
Example:
 – *will make people feel responsible for, proud of their community*
 – *will attract others to their community*
	Gives a proposal or a general suggestion
	Example:
	   involve citizens and businesses in efforts to clean up public areas in the community
	
	Offers specific solutions or ideas to solve the problem
	Example:
	   Solution 1: a yearly "clean-up" day—adults and children volunteer to clean up in different areas of the community
	
	   Solution 2: get businesses to donate money to support a community awareness program, to stop people who litter and clean up public areas

A. *Work with another student. Choose one of these problems. Brainstorm ideas to complete the problem/solution chart.*

- A student is having trouble getting to class on time.
- There is too much traffic causing accidents downtown.
- The computer lab is too crowded. There aren't enough computers for students.

Problem Section	Solution Section
Identify the problem:	Make a general proposal or suggestion:
Explain why it needs to be fixed:	Offer specific solutions or ideas to solve the problem: Solution 1: Solution 2:

B. *Join another pair and compare charts. Can you add ideas to each other's charts?*

Further Practice

Journal or Blog Topics *(See Part 1, Units 1 and 2.)*

- Choose one of the other ideas (one you did NOT use) from Exercise 5A, or use your own idea. Write a short composition (one or two paragraphs) to . . .
  - ° identify the problem and explain why it needs to be fixed.
  - ° make a general proposal or suggestion.
  - ° offer specific solutions or ideas to solve the problem.
- Read your classmates' problems and solutions and write your opinion of the problem and any other ideas you have for solutions.

Problem/Solution Essay Pattern

Problem/solution essays usually follow this basic pattern:

Introductory Paragraph

- Identifies the problem
- Explains why problem needs to be fixed
- Offers a general proposal to solve the problem (thesis statement)

Body Paragraph 1

- Explains and supports solution 1

Body Paragraph 2

- Explains and supports solution 2

Concluding Paragraph

Look at your notes from Exercise 5. Where does the information in your notes fit into the essay pattern above?

Notes:

- Problem/solution essays often also include the cause-and-effect pattern.

  Examples:

  Cause: *city has ugly, dirty public areas* → **Effect:** *people have no place to sit and enjoy the outdoors*

  Cause: *working together to help clean up areas in a city* → **Effect:** *people feel responsible and proud of their community*

- In a problem/solution paragraph, the thesis statement is usually the same as the general proposal for solving the problem.

Sorting Information—Problem/Solution Essay

In the next section you will use the 2-column chart to help you sort information for a problem/solution essay.

A. *Read a student's brainstorm for a problem/solution essay titled "Lower Stress the Healthy Way."*

- Students feel pressure to get good grades
- worry about getting jobs, into graduate school
- use "study drugs" / stimulants make brain more awake, active
- stimulants cause serious side effects
- feel stressed by amount of homework
- make a study plan
- use an assignment calendar—write down homework, exams
- at school, do not eat healthy meals like at home
- eat unhealthy snacks, junk food, sweet drinks
- eat late at night, irregular hours
- plan regular meal times
- choose healthy meals and snacks

B. *Work with another student. Are the items from Exercise A problems or solutions? Write them in the correct columns in the chart.*

Problems	Solutions

SIMPLE OUTLINES

After you have brainstormed and sorted your ideas, putting them into a simple outline will help you make a clear plan for organizing the information in your essay. Remember that your outline is not written in stone! You can continue to make any additions or changes, or change information and ideas you want to include.

EXERCISE 7

A. *Read the partial outline for the model essay "Lower Stress the Healthy Way."*

Essay Outline

Marta Silva

I. Introduction

Problem:

– students feel pressure to get good grades for jobs/graduate school
– use study drugs—can cause serious side effects

Proposal/Thesis statement:
– students need to make a study plan and eat healthily

II. Body

    A. Solution 1

        – feel stressed by studies

        – staying up late, cramming increases stress

        – keep an assignment calendar

        –

        –

    B. Solution 2

        – eat regular, healthy meals

        – first time away from home/choose junk food

        –

        –

        –

III. Conclusion

    – students can change study routines and eat a healthy diet

---

B. *Read the student's essay. Notice the bold transitions for problem/solution and cause/effect patterns.*

Marta Silva

Modern Psychology

Lower Stress the Healthy Way

In a recent study, up to 25 percent of students said they had used stimulants called "cognitive enhancers" to help them study and achieve better grades. Cognitive enhancers are stimulants—a type of drug that **causes** the brain to feel more awake or active. Many students feel pressure to get good grades in order to get jobs or be accepted into graduate programs. However, students do not realize the dangerous side effects these drugs **produce**, including disrupted sleep, moodiness, and loss of appetite. Students need to know they can lower their stress and succeed academically by making a study plan and eating right.

Many students feel stressed by the amount of schoolwork they have. **As a result**, cognitive enhancers can become a big temptation. Often, students find themselves staying up late to finish homework assignments or cramming all night for a big test the next day. This method of studying only increases students' worries and stress about grades. However, **there is a way** for students to manage their studies—keeping an assignment calendar. With an assignment calendar, students can simply fill in the due dates for homework assignments, papers, and exams. Then, students just need to make sure to check it daily and plan their time accordingly. With an assignment calendar, students can study more effectively and with less pressure. In the end, this will help them get better grades.

Another idea that can help students lower stress is to watch what they eat. For many, this is their first time away from home, where they ate healthy meals each day. At school, many students choose junk food or sweet, caffeinated drinks to give them the extra energy they need right before a class or a long night of studying at the library. However, eating unhealthy food late at night, or at irregular times can **have the opposite effect**. Luckily, in the United States, most universities have dining halls that offer healthy meals, snacks, and beverages available to students

(continued)

throughout the day. Students can plan regular meal times and purchase healthy snacks to eat when the dining hall is not open. Eating right and regularly is possible for students if they make it a priority.

In conclusion, today's college students face enormous pressure to do well in school. Many of them feel they cannot compete without study drugs. However, students can reduce stress and raise their overall grades without stimulants if they change their study routines and eat a healthy diet. **If** students do not learn how to reach their goals without cognitive enhancers, they may suffer serious, long-lasting **consequences**.

C. *Complete the outline in Exercise A on page 176 with supporting details from the essay.*

D. *Work with another student. Discuss these questions. Write your answers.*

1. How many paragraphs are in the essay? _____

2. What kind of hook is used in the introduction? _____

3. Which sentences in the introduction explain the problem? _____

   _____

   _____

4. Which sentence in the introduction expresses why it is important to stop

   the problem? _____

5. What is the thesis statement (proposal to solve the problem)? _____

   _____

6. According to the thesis statement, what will the first body paragraph be about?

   What will the second body paragraph be about? _____

   _____

7. Underline the restated thesis statement in the conclusion. How is it different from

   the thesis statement in the introduction? _____

8. What kind of final comment does the writer use in the conclusion (warning,

   suggestion, recommendation, question)? _____

WRITING TASK

Follow the steps to write a first draft of a cause/effect or a problem/solution essay:
- Brainstorm about the topic
- Organize and sort ideas
- Write an outline
- Write a first draft

A. *Work with another student. Read the list of essay topics. Which pattern best fits each one? Write CE (cause/effect) or PS (problem/solution). Both may be possible in some cases.*

_____ **1.** How weather affects people's moods

_____ **2.** Ways teachers can prevent students from cheating

_____ **3.** Advantages and disadvantages of moving to a new city

_____ **4.** Advice for staying organized

_____ **5.** How to avoid overeating

_____ **6.** An experience or an event that changed you or your life

_____ **7.** Tips for getting along with difficult people

_____ **8.** How advertising influences children

_____ **9.** Results of climate change

_____ **10.** Consequences of sleep loss

_____ **11.** How studying English has affected your life

_____ **12.** What to do about rising university costs

B. *Choose one of the topics from Exercise A. On a separate piece of paper, do a brainstorm about the topic. Use one of the brainstorming techniques from Unit 5 (listing, clustering, group discussion, and so on).*

C. *Sort and organize your ideas into a two-column chart of causes and effects or problems and solutions.*

D. *Write a thesis statement for your essay.*

E. *Use your notes to make a simple outline. Make sure it follows the appropriate essay pattern for your essay type. (See cause/effect patterns on page 168 and problem/ solution on page 172.)*

F. *Use your outline to write the first draft of your essay. Use transitions where appropriate.*

Notes:
- Keep your essay to use in Unit 8, Revising and Proofreading.
- Remember that you can change or add information to your outline and your essay as you write.

Check Your Writing

A. *Use this form to check your own essay, or exchange essays with another student and check each other's writing.*

Essay Checklist

The essay . . .

1. is a **cause/effect** or **problem/solution** essay.   (Circle one.)

2. follows the correct pattern for the essay type.   ☐

   For a cause/effect essay, circle the pattern the essay follows: A B C

3. has a thesis statement that covers the main point of the essay.   ☐

4. includes enough supporting details.   ☐

5. includes transitions.   ☐

6. has a conclusion that restates the thesis statement in different words.   ☐

7. What changes do you suggest to improve the essay?

   _____

   _____

   _____

   _____

B. *Do NOT make changes to your essay yet. Check your writing for grammar, spelling, and punctuation errors, and make notes for possible changes. (You will make changes to your essay in Unit 8.)*

UNIT 8 Revising and Proofreading

To revise means to re-*view* or re-*see* what you have written. Revision is usually the final step of the writing process and gives you the opportunity to refine and polish your writing. In academic writing, you may write two or more drafts before you turn in your final work to your teacher.

Important note: For this unit, you will need the first draft of your essay from Unit 7 or the first draft of another piece of writing.

Warm Up

Work with another student. Think about the last writing assignment you did. Discuss these questions:

- About how much time did you spend writing your first draft including prewriting and organizing?

- What was the most difficult part of the assignment? The easiest?

- How did you check your writing for errors?

- How many drafts did you write?

REVISION STRATEGIES

The purpose of revising—writing more than one draft—is to make a piece of writing more interesting, smoother, and clearer for the reader.

The process of revision may involve:

Adding
Moving
Deleting
Rewriting
$\left.\right\}$ words, phrases, paragraphs, or entire sections of a piece of writing.

Writers use several strategies to help them in the revision stage. These strategies may include:

- **Self-reviews**—a checklist to make sure your paper is as clear and accurate as you can make it

- **Feedback from a teacher and peers**—the response from your readers and their suggestions for improving your essay

The last step of the revision stage is **proofreading**. When you proofread, you read every word carefully and correct your grammar, spelling, and punctuation mistakes.

Self Reviews

Students often skip this phase of the writing process. Before you hand in your paper to your teacher or share it with your classmates, you need to check it carefully yourself to make sure you have communicated your ideas as clearly, fully, and accurately as possible.

EXERCISE 1

Use your essay draft from Unit 7 (or the first draft of another piece of writing). Read your essay carefully and complete the Self-Review Checklist.

Self-Review Checklist

Introduction

Does your introduction include a hook that grabs the reader's attention?	☐
Do you include some general information to give your readers a basic understanding of the topic?	☐
Is there a thesis statement?	☐
Does the thesis statement explain the main purpose and intent of the essay?	☐

Body

Are the paragraphs indented? If not, is there a space between paragraphs?	☐
Do all of your sentences relate to and support your thesis statement?	☐
Do your body paragraphs have one main idea?	☐
Are there enough details and examples to support your ideas?	☐
Do your ideas follow a logical order?	☐
Are all of the sentences relevant?	☐
Does the essay use transitions that are appropriate for the pattern?	☐

Conclusion

Does your conclusion restate the thesis?	☐
Does your restated thesis use different words from those that were used in the introduction?	☐
Does your conclusion briefly mention your main points?	☐
Is there a final statement or opinion about your topic?	☐
Is your conclusion free of new ideas?	☐

Errors

Did you check your writing for grammar, spelling, and punctuation errors?	☐

Which errors do you need help with? _____

_____

_____

Peer Response

In addition to advice from your teacher about how to improve your writing, you can also get help and feedback from a peer—a classmate or another student.

A peer can tell you whether your writing interested him or her, whether there were any sections or sentences he or she didn't understand, as well as give you suggestions for additional points to include.

You may have already done this kind of review for some of your writing assignments in this course.

EXERCISE 2

A. *Imagine that the first draft of the essay below is from a classmate.*
- Read the essay once.
- Read it again. Circle any errors and underline any sentences or sections you don't understand.
- Mark any suggestions or ideas to improve the essay.

Jee-Min Kim
Sociology 101
Professor Granby
November 23, 2012

Character Education

Are students more disrespectful today than in the past? Many schools report that there are more fight bad language, and disrespectful behavior than in previous years. Ramsey High School decided students needed more than some regular courses, so they added another class to the curriculum.

In the first character education class students focused on the definition of respect was. At the start, many of the students seemed uninterested and did not want to be in the class. Some of the students were more interested in the art club because they liked to draw. The leader began by asking students what respect was. Then, the leader asked the students in what situations they had seen or experienced respect. Students discussed that respect was having a high regard for others and use good manners. Students thought about the way they spoke to their grandparents or to an important person. Next, the leader asked students to think about how they spoke to there grandparents as opposed to their friends or

(continued)

teachers. They said they never argued with there grandparents or showed anger towards them. Finally, students did role plays. In the role plays, they could only use acceptable language. They also had to stop talking if the conversation became an argument.

In addition, the class studied tolerance. The students watch a movie about a teen who was treated badly by her classmates. The class talked about the same thing happening in their school and wrote about it in a journal.

To conclude, caracter education classes may be the solution for teaching students about acceptable behavior in school. Parents should also teach their children about good maners and respect. If students treat everyone respectfully, it will help them inside and outside of the classroom.

B. *Complete the Peer Response form for the essay in Exercise A.*

Peer Response Form

Your name: _____   Writer's name: _____

Date: _____

1. What is the essay topic? _____

2. What kind of hook does the writer use? Is it effective for grabbing the reader's attention? _____

3. Can you identify the thesis statement? According to the thesis statement, what specific areas or main points will the essay cover? _____

4. Does the writer present in a logical order that is easy to understand? What questions do you have? _____

5. Do the body paragraphs contain enough details, explanations, or reasons to support the main idea? What other details could the writer include? _____

6. What suggestions do you have to improve the essay?

_____

_____

_____

C. *Compare forms with another student. Discuss any differences.*

A. *Work with another student. Exchange the first draft of your essay from Unit 7 (or another piece of writing).*
- Read the essay once.
- Read it again. Circle any errors and underline any sentences or sections you don't understand.
- Mark any suggestions or ideas to improve the essay.

B. *Complete the Peer Response form for your partner's essay.*

Peer Response Form

Your name: _____ Writer's name: _____

Date: _____

1. What is the essay topic? _____

2. What kind of hook does the writer use? Is it effective for grabbing the reader's attention?
_____

3. Can you identify the thesis statement? According to the thesis statement, what specific areas or main points will the essay cover? _____

4. Does the writer present in a logical order that is easy to understand? What questions do you have? _____
_____

5. Do the body paragraphs contain enough details, explanations, or reasons to support the main idea? What other details could the writer include? _____
_____

6. What is missing or unclear in the essay? What information needs to be added? Deleted? Moved?
_____
_____
_____

7. What do you like about the essay? _____
_____

8. What other suggestions do you have to improve the essay?
_____

REVISING YOUR FIRST DRAFT

After you have completed a self-review and a peer response, you are ready to begin revising your first draft.

In your revision, you may do all or some of the following:

Add
Move
Delete
Rewrite
} words, phrases, paragraphs, or sections of your essay.

EXERCISE 4

A. *Work with another student. On page 187 look at the revisions to the first two paragraphs of the essay from Exercise 2.*

Notice the following revisions:

- Added words, phrases, and sentences are highlighted
- Deleted words, phrases, and sentences are crossed out.
- Moved words, phrases, and sentences have [brackets]

B. *Compare the writer's revisions to your suggestions from the peer response in Exercise 2B. Did the writer include any of your ideas? Tell the class which ones.*

C. *What suggestions or questions do you have to help improve the final draft of the essay? Write them here. Then compare your work with another student.*

_____

_____

_____

Jee-Min Kim
Sociology 101
Professor Granby
November 25, 2012

Character Education

Are students more disrespectful today than in the past? Many schools report that there are more fights, bad language, and disrespectful behavior than in previous years. To deal with the problem, one local school, Ramsey High School, added a special new course called Character Education to teach students about respect.

In the first character education class, students focused on the definition of respect ~~was~~. ~~At the start, many of the students seemed uninterested and did not want to be in the class. Some of the students were more interested in the art club because they liked to draw.~~ The leader began by asking students what respect was. [Students discussed that respect was having a high regard for others and using good manners.] Then, the leader asked the students in what situations they had seen or experienced respect. Students thought about the way they spoke to their grandparents or to an important person. Next, the leader asked students to think about how they spoke to their grandparents as opposed to their friends or teachers. They said they never argued with their grandparents or showed anger towards them. However, with friends they often argued or spoke in an angry way. They also said they sometimes behaved this way towards teachers. Finally, students did role plays. In the role plays, they could only use acceptable language. They also had to stop talking if the conversation became an argument. They were surprised by the results. Their conversation was friendlier, and they felt better about each other.

Use the peer response form and any other suggestions you have received to begin revising your essay from Unit 7 (or the piece of writing you have used for this unit). Follow these instructions. Try to do as many as you can:

1. Move one or more phrases, sentences, or sections. Write them here:

   _____

   _____

2. Rewrite or change one or more sentences. Write down the sentence(s) you changed.

   _____

   _____

(continued)

3. Add one or more sentences. Write down the sentence(s) you added.

_____

_____

4. Delete one or more sentences. Write down the sentence(s) you deleted.

_____

_____

5. Read your second draft. How have these changes improved your essay?

_____

_____

PROOFREADING

Often, writers wait until after they have finished revising the content of their writing before they concentrate on proofreading or correcting grammatical and formatting errors.

You are able to find and correct many errors in English, even though you are still learning. Here are some useful tips to help you with your proofreading.

Guidelines for Proofreading

- If you used a computer to type your essay, use the spell check feature first. Then proofread it yourself.

- Read each sentence slowly, one at a time.

- Read the essay once, focusing just on spelling and grammar.

- Read it again, focusing on punctuation.

- Read backwards—that is from the end to the beginning of the essay. This will help you focus on each word.

- Proofread one more time. You'll be surprised how many errors you missed.

One useful strategy for proofreading is to try to "hear" your errors. You do this by reading your essay aloud and listening for anything that doesn't sound right. Reading your writing aloud can help you find errors you miss when you silently read your essay.

A. *Read aloud your revised essay or writing assignment from Exercise 5. When you "hear" a mistake, circle it.*

B. *Read the essay again silently. Use this proofreading checklist to look for grammar, spelling, and punctuation errors. Correct as many mistakes as you can.*

Proofreading Checklist

Language Use

The essay uses appropriate language (formal vs. informal register, full forms vs. contractions, and so on).	☐

Grammar and Structure

All sentences are complete sentences.	☐
The subjects and verbs in all sentences agree.	☐
Verb tenses are used correctly.	☐
There are no run-on sentences or comma splices.	☐
The first line of each paragraph is indented, or there is a space between paragraphs.	☐

Punctuation

Each sentence begins with a capital letter.	☐
Names of people and places are capitalized.	☐
Each sentence ends with the correct punctuation.	☐
Commas and semicolons are used correctly.	☐

Spelling

I checked the spelling of the names of people and places.	☐
I used the correct spelling of words that sound alike but have different spellings and meanings (*to, two, too, there, their,* and so on).	☐
I checked the spelling of words that are new to me.	☐

Note: Do you know the kinds of mistakes you make often? Create your own proofreading checklist using the one above, and adding your common errors. You can continue to use it to help you find and correct errors in your future writing.

Timed Essays

For a timed essay, you need to complete an essay on an assigned topic or question within a given time limit. Depending on the purpose of the essay, you may have from 30 minutes to three hours to complete it.

Timed essays are often used as exams in college and university classes. Teachers use them to test students' knowledge about an area of study and to evaluate their writing skills. In classes where students are learning English, the purpose of the essay may be to check students' English levels or abilities. Many colleges and universities in English-speaking countries give essay tests to students who wish to enroll. A university may use its own test, a standard test like the TOEFL® or IELTS exam, or it might require both.

Because they have a strict time limit, skills for writing timed essays are different from those you need to write for longer class assignments. Typically, you have very little time to review and revise your work; you must work alone, and you are graded on how completely you answered the prompt.

In this unit, you will learn strategies for timed essays, including:

- Understanding essay prompts
- Planning and organizing
- Writing introductions and conclusions
- Checking and revising

Warm Up

A. *Do these statements describe timed essays, regular essay assignments, or both?*
   *Mark them **T** for timed essays, **R** for regular assignments, or **B** for both.*

_____ 1. You must work alone.

_____ 2. The introduction and conclusion are short.

_____ 3. You can write several drafts.

_____ 4. You should cite sources to support your opinions and ideas.

_____ 5. You don't have much time to review and revise your work.

_____ 6. Your grade depends on how clearly you express your ideas.

_____ 7. You can only write one, or sometimes two, drafts.

_____ 8. You may work with one or more other people.

_____ 9. You have to think very quickly.

_____ 10. It is important to understand and carefully follow the directions.

- Have you written timed essays in your own language? In English? If so, in which classes? How long did you have to complete them?

- In what classes or situations might you need to write timed essays in the future?

- What do you think is easy about writing timed essays in English? What is challenging?

ESSAY PROMPTS

A **prompt** is a statement or a question to which you write a response. There is a variety of different types of essay prompts. Depending on the essay prompt, you may be asked to . . .

- write a description.
- tell a story from personal experience.
- give your opinion.
- compare objects, ideas, or people.
- describe a process.
- explain causes and effects.

Because you need to be able to think and organize your ideas quickly for a timed essay, it is important to read the instructions very carefully and make sure you understand them fully. Then you can begin to brainstorm what to include in your essay.

EXERCISE 1

A. *Match these common instruction words from timed essay tests with their meanings.*

Instruction Words	Meanings
_____ **1.** Choose	**a.** to give the meaning of a word or concept
_____ **2.** Compare	**b.** to prove with examples, facts, and reasons
_____ **3.** Contrast	**c.** to give details that make the meaning clear
_____ **4.** Define	**d.** to select from two or more options
_____ **5.** Discuss	**e.** to describe similarities and differences between two or more things
_____ **6.** Explain	**f.** to list or identify
_____ **7.** Name	**g.** to talk about the important aspects of an issue or idea
_____ **8.** Support	**h.** to describe differences between two or more things

B. *Compare answers with another student.*

A. *Read these essay prompts for a 30-minute timed essay. Check (✓) the features and information you think would be most important to include in the essay. (Note that answers can vary.)*

1.

> Should first-year university students be required to live on campus in dormitories? Support your opinion with reasons and examples.

☐ a comparison of the costs of living in a dorm and living in an apartment

☐ a detailed description of your own dorm room

☐ three benefits of living in a dorm

☐ three disadvantages to living in a dorm

☐ a comparison of high school students and university students

☐ a comparison of university dorms in your country and dorms in the United States

☐ a funny story about your university roommate

☐ a short history of the dorms at your university

☐ a statement explaining your university's rules about where first-year students should live

2.

> What small changes in your city or town could have a positive effect on people's lives? List at least three specific ideas for changes and discuss the effects they would have. Support your response with examples.

☐ the history of your city or town

☐ a list of several problems in your city or town

☐ the name and address of the mayor of your city

☐ one idea for a change that would have a positive effect

☐ two ideas for changes that would have positive effects

☐ three ideas for changes that would have positive effects

☐ four ideas for changes that would have positive effects

☐ specific examples of positive effects you think the changes would have

☐ an example of a change that would have a negative effect on people's lives

☐ reasons why your ideas would have a positive effect

3.

> Choose an example of recent technology. Compare and contrast it with old technology, for example, a cell phone and a "landline" telephone. Explain both the positive and negative aspects of each.

☐ a list of many different examples of new and old types of technology

☐ one example of recent technology and old technology

☐ similarities between the new and the old technology

☐ differences between the new and the old technology

☐ an explanation of why you prefer the old technology

☐ the good and bad points of the new technology

☐ the good and bad points of the old technology

☐ information about when and where the old technology was first invented

☐ a comparison of the cost of the new and the old technology

☐ reasons why many people are afraid to try new technology

B. *Compare answers with another student. Explain your choices.*

ORGANIZING YOUR TIMED ESSAY

For timed essays, you need to be able to quickly organize your thoughts and ideas. Some students feel that because there is a time limit, they shouldn't spend time making an outline.

However, taking a little time to write a brief outline of your ideas is important for the following reasons:

1. It will help you decide what you want to say.
2. You will avoid leaving out any important information or details.
3. Essays are often graded on how clearly they are organized.

Your outline can be very brief—just the main ideas. If you have 30 minutes to write an essay, you should spend no more than five minutes thinking about the information you want to include and writing a brief outline

EXERCISE 3

A. *Read the following essay prompt. Then look at the samples of two students' outlines for the essay.*

<u>**U.S. History**</u>

<u>**Mid-term Exam**</u>

Should the state flag of Connecticut be redesigned? Why or why not? Use examples of historical facts and events to support your opinion.

Outline 1

      I. Intro: Should not be redesigned
     II. Tradition—official design since 1897
   III. Each symbol has special meaning
         A. grape vines
         B. motto
         C. colors
    IV. Too expensive to change
     V. Conclusion: good flag, don't change

Outline 2

   I. Flag should be redesigned
  II. Not attractive, too similar to other state flags
 III. Meanings not clear to most citizens
 IV. Change—citizens would be prouder of more attractive flag
     with clear meaning

Guidelines for Organizing Timed Essays

To organize your essay quickly:

- Write your outline on a separate piece of paper or in the margins of your exam answer sheet.
- Copy the main points from your outline onto your exam answer sheet, leaving enough room between them to fill in your discussion.
- Write just the topic sentence of each paragraph. This way, even if you run out of time and can't completely explain all your ideas, you will still be able to demonstrate your knowledge of the topic. An example of this is given on page 196.

B. *Look at the beginning of the student's essay. Which outline from page 195 will be developed?*

<u>**U.S. History**</u>
<u>**Mid-term Exam**</u>
<u>**Essay Answer Sheet**</u>

Should the state flag of Connecticut be redesigned?
Why or why not? Use examples of historical facts and events to support your opinion.

There are three main reasons why the state flag of Connecticut should not be redesigned.

First, the flag was designed in 1897 and is part of an important state tradition.

Secondly, each part of the design has a specific important meaning. For example, the three grapevines in the center are symbols of peace and good luck. They also represent

The motto,

The flag's colors

Finally, it would cost a lot of money to create new flags, and change the design on official documents and buildings. For example,

The current Connecticut flag is a good symbol for the state and should not be changed.

C. *Read the information the student added to support the essay. Write the phrases and sentences in the correct places in the essay.*

- the three original settlements of the state, New Haven, Saybrook, and Connecticut.

- "Qui transtulit sustinet," is Latin and means, "He who transplanted still sustains."

- It is a key symbol of Connecticut's history and culture.

- The flag represents tradition, its symbols have special meanings, and it would cost too much to make the change.

- were chosen by Governor O. William Coffin, who felt the blue background represented honor.

- on court papers, business cards and letterhead, and in police stations and government offices.

A. Read these essay prompts. Then write a brief outline for each one on a separate piece of paper. Spend no more than five minutes on each one. Your teacher will time you.

1. Should your country's flag be redesigned? Give reasons to support your opinion.

2. Name a subject or class you disliked in high school. Do you think it became useful in your life after high school? Why or why not?

3. Discuss two values you learned from family members that are an important part of your character. Give examples to show how these values guide you and your life.

4. Compare and contrast two works of art. They may be books, poems, songs, paintings, sculptures. Include a thesis statement and details to support your response.

5. Define "a lie" and explain whether you think it is ever acceptable to tell a lie. Support your opinion with details and examples.

B. Compare outlines with another student. How are they the same? How are they different?

TIMED ESSAY INTRODUCTIONS AND CONCLUSIONS

Introductions for timed essays are short. You may not have time to think of a clever, interesting hook or to include too much background information. It's acceptable to simply answer the question directly and spend most of your time on the body of your essay.

Conclusions can also be short and simple—just a few sentences to summarize your opinion, make a prediction, or recommend an action.

A. *Read these sample introductions for the timed essay, "Should the state flag of Connecticut be redesigned?" Check (✓) the one you think is best for a timed essay.*

☐ **Introduction 1**

The State of Connecticut was admitted to the United States as its fifth state in 1788. However, for over 100 years, the state had no official flag. The first proposal for a state flag was submitted to the state government in 1895, and a special committee was appointed to study the design. Two years later, the design was accepted and made official. The flag features a white shield with a gold and silver border, with a design of three grapevines in the center. Underneath the shield is the Latin motto "Qui Transtulit Sustinet," which means "He who transplanted still sustains." The background color of the flag is blue. This is a very attractive flag with a lot of history and symbolic meaning, and I don't think its design should be changed.

☐ **Introduction 2**

I disagree with this statement: The flag of Connecticut should be redesigned.

☐ **Introduction 3**

The state flag of Connecticut should not be changed because its current design has a long tradition, its designs have a special meaning, and it would be too expensive to replace it with a new design.

B. *Compare your choice with another student. Explain your reasons.*

Read these sample conclusions for the timed essay "Should the state flag of Connecticut be redesigned?" Check (✓) the one you think is best for a timed essay.

☐ **Conclusion 1**

In conclusion, let's change the flag.

☐ **Conclusion 2**

To sum up, the current flag design isn't very attractive. I didn't even know those were grapevines until someone told me in class. The blue isn't very special because so many other state flags use almost the same color. It's a common assignment in elementary school for children to draw their state flag, and I don't know any child who can draw such a difficult and complex flag so that anyone can recognize it. Also, most people have no idea what these symbols mean. Grapes aren't grown in Connecticut. Most people have forgotten about the three colonies that they are supposed to symbolize. Why do we have a motto in Latin, instead of in English? Even when it's translated, its meaning is not very clear. So in conclusion, I think we need a new and better flag design.

☐ **Conclusion 3**

Connecticut's flag design is unattractive and ordinary, and almost nobody knows what its symbols mean. For these reasons, I recommend a change to a simpler, more modern design for a new state flag.

EXERCISE 7

A. *Choose two of the essay prompts from Exercise 4. Write a simple introduction and conclusion for each one. Use your outlines from Exercise 4 to help you.*

B. *Compare your work with another student.*

CHECKING AND REVISING TIMED ESSAYS

As with any graded piece of writing, it's important to check and revise your essay before you hand it in. In a timed essay situation, you may have very little time to do this. Here are some useful tips for checking your work quickly and efficiently.

Guidelines for Reviewing Timed Essays

- Read the prompt again. Make sure you answered it completely. Did you include everything that the prompt asked for?
- Read each sentence to make sure you didn't leave any words out or make any simple errors.
- Change or revise vocabulary or phrases if you think of a way to express your ideas more clearly or precisely. Check for run-on sentences.
- Add any details or examples that help support your points. Delete any sentences that are unrelated to the topic.

Note: If your essay is handwritten, you can erase or cross out information and rewrite it neatly above or in the margin. Write an asterisk (*) in the margin to add information and draw an arrow to show where it should be inserted in the text.

EXERCISE 8

A. **You will have five minutes to check and revise the essay on the next page. (Your teacher will time you.)**
   Follow the guidelines above.
   Write any changes directly in your book.
   Draw an asterisk (*) where you would add this sentence in the essay:

   Nobody that I interviewed at the state governor's office was able to explain its meaning, however.

U.S. History

Mid-term Exam

Jared Sokolov

The state flag of Connecticut should be redesigned because it does not attractive, and what it symbolizes is not clear to the majority of people living here.

The flag features a central shield with three grape vine growing in the middle. However, the vines are so small that most people cannot tell what they are. The shield border is also too complex. Underneath the shield is a banner with the state motto, but unless you are very close the words is too small to read. If you look at the flag from any distance, it is difficult to tell what the picure is on this busy, confusing design. If you asked the average Connecticut citizen to draw a picture of his or her state flag, he or she would probably be unable to do it. Drawing the state flag, in fact, is a common assignment in both art and historical classes in schools. I'm sure the children wish, like I did when I was younger, for a clear, simple design!

Complex or hard-to-draw simbols might be OK if they had a strong clear meaning. However, the grapevine's have little meaning for anyone today. They represent the first three colonies (New Haven, Saybrook, and Connecticut) that joined together to make up the state of Connecticut. Is this the most important thing about our state today? I think a symbol of our geography or major products would be more meaningful. For my research on the flag, I telephoned the governor's office to ask about the flag design. A staff worker there told me that the designs around the outside of the shield actually oak leaves. But since they do not looked like oak leaves, most people do not know that. I asked about the motto, which is in Latin—even though Latin is not spoken in Connecticut and never was. The staff worker had to check on the Internet to find the English translation, "He who transplanted still sustains."

Connecticut's flag design is unattractive and ordinary, and almost nobody knows what its symbols mean. For these reasons, I recommend a change to a simpler, more modern design for a new state flag.

B. **Work in a group. Compare your revisions to the essay. Did you all find the same errors?**

A. *Choose one of your outlines from Exercise 4 for which you have written an introduction and a conclusion. Now write the body paragraphs. Spend no more than twenty minutes. (Your teacher will time you.)*

B. *Now spend five more minutes to check and revise your work. Follow the guidelines on page 200.*

WRITING TASK

Write a thirty-minute timed essay.

A. *Choose one of these prompts:*

- Define plagiarism and give at least two reasons why some students plagiarize.

- Do you agree with the quote "Honesty is always the best policy"? Explain why or why not and support your opinion with examples from personal experience.

B. *Prepare to write your essay. Spend five minutes writing an outline. Then write topic sentences for the main points from your outline on a separate piece of paper. Remember to leave space between them to develop your ideas.*

C. *Write the introduction, body paragraphs, and conclusion. Take twenty minutes.*

D. *Take five minutes to check and revise your essay.*

E. *Work in a group. Discuss these questions:*

- What was the easiest part about writing the essay?

- What was the most challenging part?

- Do you feel that you had enough time?

- If you had had another ten minutes, would you have done anything differently? Would you have done anything differently if the essay had not been timed—if you had had several days to write it?

- What is the most important thing for you to work on when you write timed essay exams in the future?

Further Practice

Journal or Blog Topics *(See Part 1, Units 1 and 2.)*

Practice writing timed essays. Here are some additional topics to choose from:

- Is there one book that you feel everyone should read, or a movie you feel everyone should see? Write an essay persuading people to read the book or see the movie?

- Some people feel that school cafeterias should provide low-fat and vegetarian meals to accommodate the eating habits of all students. Do you agree? Say why or why not and support your opinion.

- Define a "hero." Then name someone—living or dead—who you consider to be a hero. Explain why and give examples.

- Compare and contrast your "public self" and your "private self." What specific factors and feelings do you think cause these differences?

- During their lives, many people become involved in supporting a cause (helping young people, feeding the hungry, fighting for animal rights, and so on). What is a cause that you feel strongly about? Why? What ideas do you have for helping to improve the problem?

UNIT 1

Social Networking

Social networking is a form of socializing—meeting and communicating with other people—that happens in writing online. A social networking site is a Web site or online service that helps people connect to one another. You might use social networking to share information with family, friends, classmates, or coworkers, or to meet new people with similar interests. Examples of social networking sites popular with English-speaking people include Facebook® and Twitter®.

Warm Up

A. *Work in a group. Discuss these questions:*

- What are some reasons that people gather in groups to talk?

- Do you prefer to talk with friends one-on-one, in small groups, or at large gatherings? Why?

- Think about two or three of your closest friends. How long have you known them? How often do you see them? How often do you talk to them? What kinds of things do you talk about?

- Think about two or three of your acquaintances. How long have you known them? How often do you see them? How often do you talk to them? What kinds of things do you talk about?

- When you email or communicate with people online, do you discuss different topics than you do face-to-face?

Social Networking **207**

B. *Take a survey of your classmates (a group, or the whole class). Mark each classmate's answer with a small (✓) in the appropriate column. (You will need to add several marks in the same column.)*

Social Networking Survey			
1. How many different social networking sites do you use? Which ones are they?	None	1 or 2	3+
2. About how many friends do you have on the site you use most?	1–100	100–200	200+
3. Who are most of your online "friends"?	Old friends	Friends I also see in person	People I met online
4. How many times per week do you go online for social networking?	Once	2–3	4+
5. How many hours per week do you spend on social networking?	Less than 2	2–6	7+
6. What do you mostly use the social networking site(s) for?	Keeping in touch with old friends	Communicating about hobbies/interests	Professional networking

7. Use this space to write 2–3 interesting things you learned about or from your classmates while you did this survey.

_____

_____

_____

C. *Use the information from the survey to complete the sentences.*

1. Everyone (or almost everyone) in our class _____

2. No one in our class _____

3. Several people _____

4. About half the class _____

5. Only a few people _____

6. Most people _____

D. *On a separate piece of paper, write a paragraph about the use of social networking sites in your class. Use sentences similar to the ones in Exercise C, and include some of the interesting comments from survey question 7.*

POSTING ON SOCIAL NETWORKING SITES

There aren't any real "rules" about what—or how—to post on social networking sites. Different people have different opinions. To use social networking effectively, though, you should think about why you are using that site. What do you want to express? How would you like other people to think about you? Remember that how you present yourself will influence other people's opinions of you. Also, remember that information posted online is never truly private, and that comments you write can be shared with other people, even if you don't want them to be.

EXERCISE 1

A. *Read people's statements about social networking. Write **A** if you agree, **D** if you disagree, or **N** if you have no opinion.*

_____ 1. I post questions on my site, like "Who's your favorite actor?" or "Where would you like to go on vacation?" We get some good discussions, and it's interesting to see everybody's answers.

_____ 2. I can't stand it when people post boring stuff, like what they ate for dinner or what music they're listening to. Who cares?

_____ 3. I don't care what people post, as long as they spell it correctly! I don't have time to figure out people's mistakes and crazy abbreviations.

_____ 4. I sometimes feel bad when all my friends are posting about their successes—their salary raise at work, their new car, all the awards their kids won, photos of their fantastic vacations. It makes me feel like my own life is boring.

(continued)

_____ 5. Hey, it's the Internet, not an English assignment. I don't worry about spelling and grammar. If people can understand what I wrote, that's good enough. It takes too much time to do it all like a school assignment.

_____ 6. I often post links to stories and articles from the news that I think are important or interesting. I check out my friends' links, too—I really learn a lot that way!

_____ 7. I'm so tired of people posting links all the time! I don't care what your favorite song in high school sounds like! And who has time to go read all those long articles? If you have something to say, just sum it up in a few sentences for me, and then I might read it.

_____ 8. *Some of my friends post all the time, like three or four times a day, every day. It's too much. I can't possibly read it all, and then I miss things from my other friends.*

_____ 9. I hate it when people post controversial stuff, like political opinions. Not all of my friends share the same views, and it sometimes causes fights. I want my site to be a friendly place!

_____ 10. I have some people on my friends list now that I don't really like very much, as well as some people I don't have anything in common with. However, I feel it would be rude to remove them, so even though I wish they weren't connected to me, I don't say or do anything about it.

B. *Write a paragraph about your own social networking "posting style." Include information about the kinds of links, photos, etc., you would include. If you do not use social networking sites, write a paragraph explaining why not and say what you like and dislike about them.*

C. *Work in a group. One person collects all of the paragraphs and reads them aloud without telling the author's name. The others guess who wrote the paragraph.*

D. *Try social network posting on paper with your group. Follow these steps:*

1. On a separate piece of paper, write a short post at the top. Include your name.

2. Pass your "post" to another classmate. You don't have to pass to the person right next to you—you can choose any classmate.

3. Read the post you received and write a comment under it, with your name. Then pass it to another classmate.

4. Continue posting and passing until your teacher asks you to stop.

5. Find your original post and read all of the comments. Do you want to respond to any of them?

SOCIAL NETWORKING PROFILES

While every social networking site is a little different, these sites usually have some things in common. Most sites let users make a **profile** with some personal information—name, gender, age, job, education, hobbies and interests, and so on. Most sites let users upload photos, too.

Some people worry about putting too much personal information online because they are concerned about safety or privacy. They worry that someone could use the information to gain access to credit card or bank information, for example, because some people use information like birth dates, names of pets, and special places as passwords.

However, if you don't put any personal information at all up on your site, it may make it harder for old friends to find and contact you, or for new people to realize you have a lot in common and want to get to know you. It's important to be selective about the type and amount of personal information you choose to include.

EXERCISE 2

A. *Look at the information included on some social networking profiles. Check (✓) the information you would include on your own profile.*

- ☐ first name
- ☐ last name
- ☐ your current city
- ☐ your hometown
- ☐ home address
- ☐ email address
- ☐ cell phone number
- ☐ name of employer or school
- ☐ name of high school or university you graduated from
- ☐ name of spouse
- ☐ names of children
- ☐ photo of you

- ☐ photo of things or places you like
- ☐ hobbies or interests
- ☐ your religion
- ☐ your political party or views
- ☐ a statement of personal philosophy
- ☐ names of books, movies, and music you like
- ☐ a list of all the friends on your social networking site
- ☐ your professional résumé
- ☐ your university grades
- ☐ favorite sports teams or athletes
- ☐ favorite quotes

B. *Work in a group. Discuss your lists from Exercise A. Talk about why you would or would not include the information.*

Work with another student. Read the social networking profiles. Then discuss these questions:

- Do the profiles seem interesting to you? Why or why not?

- What do the pictures tell you about each person?

- Imagine each person asked you to suggest one change to his or her profile to make it seem more interesting. What would you suggest?

http://www.sharefriends.smac/sn.com

SHARE: POST   PHOTOS   VIDEO   LINK

Nice to meet you! I'm Seumus (say it like Shay-mus) MacLellan. College student (architecture) and saxophone player.

I'm a 3rd year architecture student who's interested in designing environmentally smart buildings for public spaces. Our cities are only going to become more crowded, so the challenge for us is to keep our communities clean and functioning smoothly. I like to think I'll be able to help with that some day.

In my free time, I'm usually listening to music or playing it. I'm a huge jazz fan. I belong to two different bands, and one of them, The Happy Campers, plays in public sometimes, so if you want our schedule, just shoot me an email.

I'm a pretty friendly guy, so I like to meet new people. If you send me a friend request, I'll probably say yes—but I'd like to know why you sent me one. Do we have something in common? Or do I just seem like an irresistibly cool guy? lol

College: Edinburgh School of the Arts, Edinburgh, Scotland

High School: Caledonia Secondary School

Email: smacclellan@writingpower.net

Introduction: Find me on my blog at http://www.jaimiewilson.com
Occupation: software developer
Employer: WP Software Systems, Inc.
Hobbies & interests: snowboarding, skiing, hiking, science fiction movies
Looking for: friends, networking
Gender: Female
Search visibility: Visible in search

When I'm not designing software, I'm heading for the mountains! I get on my snowboard every chance I get—the faster the slope, the better! I guess you could say I like living life on the edge. I'm always in search of adventure . . . Join me!

SHARE: POST PHOTOS VIDEO LINK

RECENT ACTIVITY:

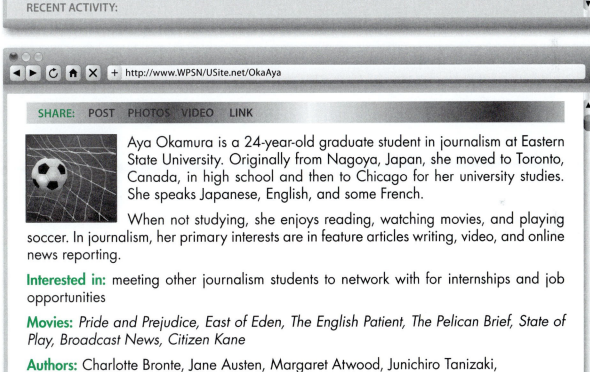

SHARE: POST PHOTOS VIDEO LINK

Aya Okamura is a 24-year-old graduate student in journalism at Eastern State University. Originally from Nagoya, Japan, she moved to Toronto, Canada, in high school and then to Chicago for her university studies. She speaks Japanese, English, and some French.

When not studying, she enjoys reading, watching movies, and playing soccer. In journalism, her primary interests are in feature articles writing, video, and online news reporting.

Interested in: meeting other journalism students to network with for internships and job opportunities

Movies: *Pride and Prejudice, East of Eden, The English Patient, The Pelican Brief, State of Play, Broadcast News, Citizen Kane*

Authors: Charlotte Bronte, Jane Austen, Margaret Atwood, Junichiro Tanizaki, Stieg Larsson

WRITING TASK

A. *Write a profile for a new social networking site. Follow these steps:*

1. Use the list in Exercise 2 to help you decide what to include.

2. Choose an image to represent yourself. Draw a picture or bring a photo or image to class.

3. Write a profile at least one paragraph long. Use the models in Exercise 3 to help you, and add your own ideas.

B. *Share your profile with a group or the whole class. Discuss these questions:*

- Was there any information that everyone (or almost everyone) included?

- Whose profile was the most different from yours?

- Did you learn anything about your classmates that you didn't already know?

UNIT 2

Business Letters

Business letters and business emails are different from types of informal writing. When writing for business situations—whether you're communicating with colleagues, inquiring about a job, or requesting information from a company—it's important to know the correct format, language, tone, and style. Generally, business writing includes some kind of purpose: You want to buy or sell something, to apply for or offer a job, to introduce yourself or your company. The correct language and style can help you achieve this purpose.

Warm Up

A. *Work in a group. Make a list of reasons that people write business letters (for example, to request information or complain about a product). Share your list with the class.*

B. *Discuss these questions with your group:*

- What types of business letters have you written? Have you written any business letters or emails in English? Have you received any in English?

- What kinds of business letters are sent mostly by email? Are they usually sent as an email, or as an attachment?

- What kinds are sent mostly on paper? Do you think this will change in the future?

- What kinds of business letters do you think you may write in the future?

BUSINESS LETTER FORMAT

Formal business letters include additional parts and usually follow a set format. This helps writers know how to organize their letter, and it helps readers find the important information.

You are probably familiar with the basic parts of a letter.

The **greeting**, or salutation, tells who you are writing to.

When you know the receiver's name, the greeting begins with the word *Dear*:

Dear Mr. Gilbert: *Dear Ms. Humphreys:*

Dear Professor Sears: *Dear Dr. Heinz:*

When you do not know the receiver's name, use one of the following greetings:

To Whom It May Concern: *Dear Sir or Madam:*

The **closing** ends the letter politely. Common business letter closings include the following:

Best wishes,   *Sincerely yours,*

Kind regards,   *Yours truly,*

Sincerely,   *Thank you for your consideration.*

> **Notes:**
> - In friendly letters, the greeting is always followed by a comma: *Dear Cathy,*
> - However, in business letters, a comma or a colon may be acceptable—*Dear Ms. Kimmel,* or *Dear Ms. Kimmel:*—depending on where you are and how formal the situation is. The colon is more formal.
> - The closing is always followed by a comma.
> - In British English, the greeting and closing are generally not followed by any punctuation.

The **signature** appears at the end of the letter. It includes your handwritten signature as well as your typed name. You may also include a job title, if you wish.

Thomas Sheldon
Thomas Sheldon
Sales Manager

The following exercises will review the other aspects of a business letter format.

A. Work with another student. Label the parts of the business letter with words from the box.

> body   date   salutation (greeting)
> closing   introduction   sender's address
> conclusion   receiver's address   signature

1427 55th Avenue NE
Seattle, WA 98105   **1.** _____

October 27, 2012   **2.** _____

Casey Krevitz, Executive Director
Middleton Symphony Orchestra
180 Midland Avenue, Suite 411   **3.** _____
Chicago, IL 60604

Dear Ms. Krevitz: **4.** _____

Xxx xxxxxxx xxxxx xxxxxxxx xxxx x xxxxxxx. xxxxxxx xx
xxxxxxx xxxxxx. Xxxxxx xxxx xxxxxxxx xxxxxxxxxx xxx   **5.** _____
xxxxx. Xxxxx x xxxxxxxxxxx xxxxx xxxxxx xxx xxxxx
xxxxxxxxxx xxxxxx xxxxxxxx.

Xxx xxxxxxx xxxxx xxxxxxxx xxxx x xxxxxxx xxxxxxx xx
xxxxxxx xxxxx x. Xxxxxx xxxx xxxxxxx xxxxxxxx xxxxx
xxxxxxxxx xxxxxxxxx xxxx. Xxxxx xxxxxxxx xxxxx xxxxxx   **6.** _____
xxxxxxx xxx. Xxxxxxx xxxx xxxxxxx xxxxx xxxx xxxxx.
Xxxxx xxxx xx xxxxxxxx xxxx xx xxxxx xxxxxxxx xx xx.
Xxx xxxxxxxxxx xxxxxx xxxxxx.

Xxx xxxxxxx xxxxx xxxxxxxx xxxxxxxx xxxx x xxxxxxx xxxxxxx xx
xxxxxxx xxxxx x. Xxxxxx xxxx xxxx xxxxxxx xxxx. X xxxxx   **7.** _____
xxxx xxxxxxx xxxx xxxxx.

Sincerely,   **8.** _____

Chris Martin   **9.** _____

B. *Work with another student. Answer these questions about the business letter in Exercise A.*

1. What do you notice about the beginning of each paragraph? Between each paragraph?

2. Which words tell you the receiver's job title? Where are these words located?

3. What organization does the receiver work for? What information comes before and after the organization's name?

4. What information tells you whether the receiver is a man or a woman?

5. Do you know whether the sender is a man or a woman? Married or single? Why or why not?

6. How many lines are skipped between the closing and the sender's typed name? Why do you think this is?

EXERCISE 2

Often in a business situation, you do not know the person you are writing to. Write the correct greeting from the box for each situation.

> Dear Mr. Smith: Dear Pat Smith:
> Dear Ms. Smith: To Whom It May Concern:

1. You know that the receiver is a woman. _____

2. You know that the receiver is a man. _____

3. You do not know any information about the person. _____

4. You know the receiver's first and last name. _____

Notes: When writing to a woman, the title *Ms.* is the most appropriate for business communication. In other situations, the titles *Mrs.* and *Miss* are also used to address women.

- *Mrs.* is sometimes used for a married woman who uses her husband's surname. Some married women prefer *Ms.*, however.

- *Miss* is generally used for a younger, unmarried woman, such as a teenager.

CONTENT OF A BUSINESS LETTER

Of course, what you write in a business letter depends on what you need to say. However, most business letters follow the same general organization:

- The **introductory paragraph** gives the reason or reasons you are writing the letter. Useful phrases for introductory paragraphs are shown in **bold**.

  Examples:

    I'm writing to inquire about *the photography contest.*

    This letter is to explain *my problem with a recent order.*

    I'm writing in response to *your email of October 27.*

    I appreciate your contacting me about *my Web site design services.*

- The **body paragraphs** give more information about the question or issue.

  Examples:

    Please send me details about the rules of the contest.

    The phone I received was not the same model I ordered.

    I gladly accept the invitation to speak to your students.

    I have created Web sites for a number of businesses in the area.

- The **concluding paragraph** thanks the receiver, requests an action, or promises an action. Useful phrases for concluding paragraphs are shown in **bold**.

  Examples:

    I look forward to your reply.

    Thank you for your attention *to this matter.*

    In closing, *I am looking forward to meeting you and your students in person.*

    I would be happy to *meet with you to discuss design and pricing.*

This organizational pattern is the same whether the business letter is sent through the mail, written in the body of an email, or sent as an email attachment.

EXERCISE 3

*Do these sentences belong in the introduction, the body, or the conclusion of a business letter? Write **I** (introduction), **B** (body), or **C** (conclusion).*

_____ **1.** I look forward to hearing from you.

_____ **2.** My marketing professor, Dr. Sadia Azzan, recommended that I contact you about an internship at Sparkles Media, Inc.

_____ **3.** This letter is in response to your advertisement for a Spanish-to-English translator.

_____ **4.** Please let me know if you have any further questions.

(continued)

_____ 5. The items arrived on time, but three of them were damaged.

_____ 6. I'll be able to bring the full report to the meeting on Friday.

_____ 7. I'm a student at Western United Business College, and I'm conducting a survey on efficiency in the workplace.

_____ 8. I'll look forward to our meeting this Saturday at 10:00 A.M.

_____ 9. A second consideration is that several staff members will be on vacation that week.

_____ 10. Thank you for contacting me about my screenplay.

EXERCISE 4

A. *Rewrite these introductory and concluding sentences from business letters. Replace the underlined portions with similar phrases. Use the useful phrases in bold on page 219 and the sentences from Exercise 3 to help you.*

Introductions:

1. <u>I'm writing to ask you about</u> volunteering at your clinic this summer.

   _____

2. <u>I'm writing in response to</u> your advertisement for a part-time swim instructor.

   _____

3. <u>My professor, Dr. Kim, suggested that I contact you about</u> an article for our college newspaper.

   _____

Conclusions:

4. <u>I'll see you</u> next Thursday at 2:30.

   _____

5. <u>Thank you for your help with</u> this matter.

   _____

6. <u>I'd like to</u> meet with your design team.

   _____

B. *Write your own introductory and concluding sentences using the phrases from Exercise A.*

Introductory:

1. _____

2. _____

Concluding:

3. _____

4. _____

BUSINESS COMMUNICATION

The language of business communication is relatively formal—even if you already know and are friendly with the person you are writing to. Remember that business letters can be shared with other people in the same company. Here are some general tips for appropriate business communication:

Guidelines for Better Business Communication

- Avoid informal and personal topics. Don't include jokes, stories, or personal photographs.

- Don't use slang or abbreviations. Write out words and expressions fully.

- Use complete sentences. Occasionally, a phrase is OK, but a complete sentence will never be incorrect.

- Use formal punctuation. Begin each sentence with a capital letter, and end each sentence with a period or question mark. (Note that exclamation points are usually informal.)

A. *Work with another student. Read the business letter and answer these questions:*

- What can you say about the format of the letter? Is it a paper letter or an email?

- Which parts are too informal for business communication? Why? Use the Guidelines on page 221 to help you.

Hi Jasper!

Sorry I missed your phone call. A friend of mine from high school was in town, and we went out to lunch. After that, we went to the park because the weather was so nice. Here's a photo from my cell phone of the lake at the park. Isn't it lovely? Anyway, I got your email, so I can answer yours now.

I can come for a meeting on June 15th. Not the 20th, though. I have a dental appointment then. :(Oh, do you guys have a projector? I wanna show some slides of the building site. It's pretty cool! I checked with the conference center 2 C if they had a projector, but it was like $500 a day to rent one, which is totally crazy.

So, I have some updates to the design. I can make copies and bring some 4 everybody. Do you also want me to email a copy to you before the 15th? Then you'll be able to see the updates before the meeting. Like a sneak preview! :)

OK, I gotta lot of stuff to do today, so I should go now. I'll see ya on the 15th! Can't wait!

Bye for now,
Alex

B. *On a separate piece of paper, rewrite the letter using more formal language.*

C. *Work in a group. Take turns reading your letters aloud. How are they same? How are they different?*

EMAIL LANGUAGE

Email can be slightly less formal than traditional paper letters. However, it's important to remember that email business letters should still follow business format and tone. In addition, it's common for business emails to be forwarded to other people whom you might not know well. Therefore, keep your business emails polite and business-like at all times!

The main differences between business emails and business letters sent through the mail are:

- Emailed business letters tend to be shorter.
- People expect a response to email sooner than with mailed letters.

EXERCISE 6

A. *Read the online interview with a business expert. Underline two pieces of advice that you think are useful or important. Then share and explain your choices with another student.*

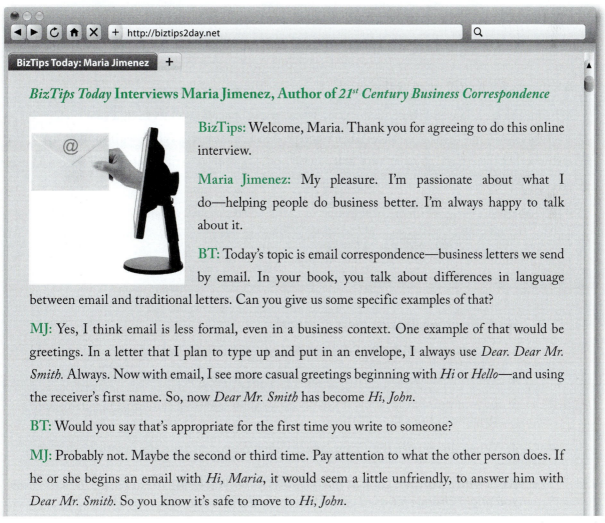

http://biztips2day.net

BizTips Today: Maria Jimenez +

BizTips Today **Interviews Maria Jimenez, Author of** *21ˢᵗ Century Business Correspondence*

BizTips: Welcome, Maria. Thank you for agreeing to do this online interview.

Maria Jimenez: My pleasure. I'm passionate about what I do—helping people do business better. I'm always happy to talk about it.

BT: Today's topic is email correspondence—business letters we send by email. In your book, you talk about differences in language between email and traditional letters. Can you give us some specific examples of that?

MJ: Yes, I think email is less formal, even in a business context. One example of that would be greetings. In a letter that I plan to type up and put in an envelope, I always use *Dear. Dear Mr. Smith.* Always. Now with email, I see more casual greetings beginning with *Hi* or *Hello*—and using the receiver's first name. So, now *Dear Mr. Smith* has become *Hi, John.*

BT: Would you say that's appropriate for the first time you write to someone?

MJ: Probably not. Maybe the second or third time. Pay attention to what the other person does. If he or she begins an email with *Hi, Maria*, it would seem a little unfriendly, to answer him with *Dear Mr. Smith.* So you know it's safe to move to *Hi, John.*

(continued)

BT: How about closings? Are they also less formal?

MJ: I see *Best wishes* followed by the full name in the signature, and then after a few exchanges, it changes to just *Best*, followed by the person's first name. One surprising thing I've seen a few times is a closing followed by nothing—just *Sincerely* or *Best wishes*, a comma, and then no name! It's really inappropriate. Even if you leave off with *Best*, you always need to end a letter with your name.

BT: That's interesting. Do you have any examples of cross-cultural differences, differences in ways people communicate by email in different countries?

MJ: It's hard to say. Sometimes I think a lot of English speakers forget that it can be a challenge to read and write in a language that isn't your first. Especially when you write an email in another language, you know that other people need to understand your message, so you want to spell everything correctly, use correct grammar. This means it might take more time to reply, and that can make some people impatient.

BT: And . . . what's the solution to that?

MJ: To communicate and let people know what's going on. Just send back a quick note that says *I received your email, and I'll answer by Friday.* Just make sure you pick a realistic date, and then stick to it!

BT: Thank you for that tip. Any closing advice? Just one thing.

MJ: One thing . . . I guess I'll choose this one: Always use your spell-checker! Even if your spelling is very good, it's easy to make mistakes when you type. Most email services come with an automatic spell-checker these days, so make sure that's turned on. Or you can write your email in a word processing program, check it, and then paste it into email.

BT: Thank you, Maria. For more of this kind of useful advice, as well as sample business emails and letters, don't forget to pick up a copy of Maria's book, *21st Century Business Correspondence*, available in print and as an e-book through the links at the bottom of this page.

B. *Work in a group. Discuss these questions:*

1. Do you agree with all of the advice in the interview?

2. Can you think of any other suggestions for writing business emails?

3. In your opinion, when is it OK to forward an email without asking permission? When is it not OK?

4. When do you use the *Cc* function? When do you use the *Bcc* function?

C. *Work with a partner. Look at the business letter you wrote in Exercise 5. Discuss how you might change it based on the advice in the interview.*

WRITING TASK

A. *Think of a company or organization you know. Plan a business letter; for example, to ask for information, order a product, complain, or make a positive comment. Complete the chart with your ideas.*

Reason for Writing (appointment, complaint, information request, ordering product or service)	Email Letter or Paper Letter?	Receiver's Name and Company	Greeting/Closing

B. *Write your letter on a separate piece of paper. Use your own address or a realistic one from your country. Then type or email your letter (to yourself, to a classmate, or to your teacher) and print a copy.*

Check Your Writing

A. *Use this form to check your own letter, or exchange letters with another student and check each other's writing.*

Business Letter Checklist

1. The letter includes . . .

- the sender's address. ☐
- the date. ☐
- the receiver's address. ☐
- a greeting. ☐
- an introductory paragraph. ☐
- body paragraph(s). ☐
- a concluding paragraph. ☐
- a closing. ☐
- a signature. ☐

2. The letter follows the correct format. ☐

3. The letter uses formal tone and language. ☐

4. The writer avoids slang and abbreviations. ☐

5. The writer uses complete sentences and correct grammar. ☐

6. The writer uses correct punctuation for business letters. ☐

7. What changes do you suggest to improve the letter?

_____

_____

_____

_____

_____

B. *Make changes to improve your letter. Remember to check your writing for grammar, spelling, and punctuation errors.*

UNIT 3

Writing Reviews

You have probably read reviews of products, businesses, and services online or in a newspaper. Perhaps you have even written reviews yourself. Consumers write reviews to evaluate goods they have purchased or services they have experienced. They may write reviews of movies and books, restaurants and hotels, or even of classes they have taken.

Potential customers read these reviews to help them decide if they want to buy a particular product (see a movie, take a class, eat at a restaurant, and so on). For this reason, it's important for reviews to contain enough useful information and examples. Good reviews contain factual information as well as personal opinions and impressions. Writing a clear, useful review is a way for you to share your experiences with other people, and provide a valuable service to them.

Warm Up

Work in a group. Discuss these questions:

- How often do you read reviews for products and services (electronics, restaurants, shops, movies)? Where do you read them?

- Have you ever bought a product or used a service (or decided not to buy/use one) based on a bad review? Describe the experience.

- Have you ever written a review? What was the product or service? What did you write?

FORMAT OF A REVIEW

Reviews can be formal or informal. Many newspapers and magazines feature a review section where reporters share their opinions of products and services. These types of reviews are well researched and carefully written. On the other hand, some of the reviews posted on Web sites are less thorough.

Guidelines for Writing Reviews

A good review should . . .

- clearly identify the product or service

  ○ for a product, include the name and any other important identifying information, such as model or serial number, etc.

  ○ for a business or service, include the name, type of service, and location

- briefly describe the product or business (the type of movie/book, what the product does, what services the business offers)

- describe the reviewer's personal experience and opinion of the product

- make a recommendation (whether or not to buy or use the product or service)

- include information about where to buy the product

EXERCISE 1

A. *Work with another student. Read the online review on the next page. Number the sections of the review that do these things:*

1. describe the reviewer's experience
2. explain the product
3. make a recommendation
4. identify the product
5. say where / how to buy the product

Customer Review 1

★★★☆☆ **Not a bad printer, but has some problems**

The HexiPro 4300G is a printer made by TBR Electronics. The printer is advertised as an "all-in-one." That means it prints, scans, photocopies, and sends faxes. It's great for my home office. I chose it because it's one of the least expensive models, and the box said it would work with my computer. It's a nice, compact size, and it comes in several colors.

The instructions were simple, and the printer was pretty easy to set up. However, once I got it hooked up, it didn't work. I went back to the store and talked to someone there, but they couldn't help me. I tried to call the tech support phone number, but I just got several recorded messages, and they weren't any help. I finally did some searching on the Internet and learned that you have to download special software to connect the printer to the computer.

Now that I have the software installed, the printer works well. It's a little slow, but it's OK for a home office. It's also quiet, which is important to me. However, the scanner doesn't work very well. It often scans only part of the document, instead of the whole thing. I can fix that, but I have to adjust a lot of settings, and it takes some time. Furthermore, some of the colors aren't very bright on the scans, even though the color printing works fine. I haven't tried sending a fax yet, so I don't know how that works.

It's a pretty solid, well-made printer, but if you don't need the fax and scanner, buy just a simple printer, which would be cheaper. I wouldn't buy the HexiPro 4300G if you wanted to use the scanner a lot. Also, I wouldn't recommend this all-in-one to someone who is not good with computers. You'd have to be comfortable finding, downloading, and installing new software. You can't just plug this one in out of the box and use it immediately.

You can get this online, but shipping costs might be high. I got mine from a local store so that I could take it home the same day—which didn't help me in the end, since it didn't work that day.

B. *Compare answers with another student. Then discuss these questions:*

- What does the product do?
- What did the reviewer like about the product?
- What did the reviewer dislike?
- Was the reviewer happy with the product overall?
- Based on the review, would you buy this product? Why or why not?

DESCRIBING PRODUCTS AND SERVICES

Readers of reviews want to know what the product is really like before they decide to spend money on it. Depending on the reviewer's opinion, a product or service may be described in a positive or negative way.

Giving an accurate description of a product or service requires the right vocabulary.

Look at the review in Exercise 1. Underline the words and phrases the reviewer uses to describe the product. Then share your answers with the class.

EXERCISE 2

A. *Read the adjectives in the left column of the chart. Look up any new words in your dictionary. Then add them to your vocabulary notebook.*

B. *Work with another student. What types of products and services can each adjective describe? Check (✓) all of the possible columns.*

	Books, Movies, Video Games	Restaurant Food and Service	Computers, Cameras, Cell Phones	Travel Services (airlines, hotels)
bland				
boring				
comfortable				
compact				
confusing				
courteous				
delicious				
difficult				
dramatic				
efficient				
flimsy				
hilarious				
hi-tech				
inefficient				
innovative				

	Books, Movies, Video Games	Restaurant Food and Service	Computers, Cameras, Cell Phones	Travel Services (airlines, hotels)
pricey				
professional				
reasonable (price)				
reliable				
simple				
slow				
solid				
sturdy				
surprising				
tasty				
tedious				
thorough				
thrilling				
well-made				

C. *Work with another student. Discuss each word in Exercise A. Does the word give a positive or a negative description?*

D. *Join another pair. On a separate piece of paper, list four or five more words to describe the products and services in Exercise A. Try to think of both positive and negative words. Then share them with the class.*

MAKING RECOMMENDATIONS

Most readers want a review to directly answer the question: *Should I . . . ?*

Should I . . .
watch this movie?
stay at this hotel?
read this book?
buy this camera?
eat at this restaurant?
trust this mechanic?
use this online airline reservation service?

Recommendations usually use direct language. They can be short simple sentences.

Examples:

Don't buy this laptop!

I recommend the Snappy Snack Shack.

They can also include a reason in the sentence with the recommendation.

Examples:

Don't buy this laptop if you want a computer that works with video games.

I recommend the Snappy Snack Shack for cheap, delicious sandwiches and shakes.

Useful Words and Phrases for Making Recommendations	
Positive	**Negative**
Try/Buy . . . I (highly) recommend . . . You won't regret buying/using . . . I encourage anyone to buy/try . . .	Don't buy/use . . . I don't recommend . . . I wouldn't suggest buying/using . . . I would discourage anyone from buying/using . . .
Comparative adjectives: better, faster, more knowledgeable, etc.	**Comparative adjectives:** slower, less efficient, more confusing, etc.
Superlative adjectives: the best, the most reliable, the cheapest, etc.	**Superlative adjectives:** the worst, the least effective, the lowest quality, etc.

At the end of a recommendation, reviewers usually give a general summary of their opinion of the product. Often a review mentions both positive and negative aspects in the body of the review, so the reader will appreciate a clear, final recommendation in the conclusion.

Useful Phrases for Summarizing Recommendations	
Overall . . .	In conclusion, . . .
In general/Generally, . . .	On the whole, . . .
All in all . . .	All things considered, . . .

A. Work with another student. Read the recommendations.

On the first line, write "+" if the recommendation is positive. Write "–" if it is negative.

On the second line, write S if the recommendation expresses a strong opinion (positive or negative), and W if the recommendation expresses weaker feeling.

_+_ _S_ **1.** Without a doubt, the best book I've read this year. I highly recommend it.

____ ____ **2.** If you need a sturdy pair of hiking boots at a reasonable price, try Sam's Camping Supply.

____ ____ **3.** I wouldn't watch _Cowboy Sunrise_ again if it was the last movie on earth.

____ ____ **4.** In conclusion, if you like spicy food and creative dishes, you'll enjoy dinner at Marcella's.

____ ____ **5.** I don't recommend the Hanging Gardens unless you have three hours for lunch. They have the slowest service!

____ ____ **6.** All in all, the Spinning Windmills golf course isn't the best I've seen, but it's OK for a fun afternoon with friends.

____ ____ **7.** _Cowboy Sunrise_ is definitely the best movie you'll see this year.

____ ____ **8.** Tinytreasure.com has well-made products and friendly service.

____ ____ **9.** This isn't a camera for a beginner, but if you know what you're doing, you'll be able to take some great photos.

____ ____ **10.** This e-book was free, and even that was too pricey. Save your money and time.

B. Underline useful words and phrases in Exercise A that you can use for giving recommendations.

A. *Work with another student. Write an example for each type of product or service. Choose examples that you both know.*

- a song or musical artist/group: _____

- a restaurant or food product: _____

- a local store: _____

- a movie or book: _____

- an online site, store, or service: _____

B. *On your own, write a short recommendation (one or two sentences) for each example on a separate piece of paper.*

C. *Compare recommendations with your partner. Do you both agree? Explain your opinions.*

VERB TENSES IN REVIEWS

Because reviews contain a mix of information and times, they also contain a mix of verb tenses. Here are some common tenses used in reviews:

Simple present: for the reviewer's general feelings; information about a product or service that is always true; general information about a book or movie

Examples:

I don't usually like spicy food.

Vampire Stories is available as a paperback or an e-book.

Stephen Lee charges $30 an hour for math tutoring.

The new model of the smartphone comes with a larger touch screen.

Simple past: for the reviewer's experiences and stories

Examples:

The service was fast, but the food was cold.

I ordered the book on September 5, but it didn't arrive until the middle of October.

After one month, the printer jammed every time I used it.

Present perfect: (most commonly) to talk about the events the reviewer hasn't experienced yet, or has already experienced, or has experienced several times

Examples:

I haven't visited their newest store at the mall yet.

I've purchased several items from this Web site.

I've never seen a cheaper camera with this many features.

Modals and Conditionals: to make recommendations and give advice

> **Examples:**
>
> *I wouldn't recommend ordering the set meal. It's too much food.*
>
> *If you don't like violent movies, you shouldn't watch* Scare Fest IV.

Imperative: to make strong recommendations or give warnings

> **Examples:**
>
> *Buy this jacket!*
>
> *Don't get* Heroes of War: Final Conflict. *It's terrible.*

EXERCISE 5

A. **Work with another student. Look again at the review on page 229. Underline the verbs.**

B. **Look at the verbs you underlined. Circle all of the verb tenses used for each part of the review. (You may circle more than one.) Then complete the summary by putting the verbs in parentheses in the same tense.**

1. identifying the product

    a. simple present   **b.** modals   **c.** simple past

    The HexiPro 4300G (be) _____ an all-in-one machine.

    It (include) _____ a printer, a fax, and a scanner.

2. explaining the product

    a. simple present   **b.** conditional   **c.** simple past

    It (print, scan, and fax) _____ .

3. describing the reviewer's experience

    a. simple present   **b.** simple past   **c.** both simple present and simple past

    The HexiPro (not come) _____ with all of the necessary

    software, so I (have to) _____ download it myself.

    Now, it (print) _____ nicely, but the scanner (not work)

    _____ very well.

4. giving a recommendation

    a. simple present   **b.** imperative   **c.** conditional

    If you are looking for a good scanner, I (not recommend) _____
    this product.

    (buy) _____ it only if you are good with computers.

WRITING TASK

For this writing task, you will write two reviews: one for a restaurant or movie, and another for a product or service.

> Writing Task 1:   Write a review of a restaurant or a movie.

A. *What factors make you decide to try a restaurant or see a movie? Check (✓) the features of a restaurant that are important to you. (You may add to the list.) Then brainstorm more features that are important when you evaluate a movie.*

Restaurant	Movie
☐ availability of parking	☐ who the actors are
☐ cleanliness	☐ quality of acting
☐ decor and atmosphere	☐ location of theater
☐ friendliness of staff	☐
☐ how crowded it is	☐
☐ how healthy the food is	☐
☐ how well-known it is	☐
☐ location	☐
☐ noise level	☐
☐ other people's recommendations	☐
☐ price	☐
☐ taste	☐
☐ type of food	☐
☐ type of music playing	☐
☐ variety of food	☐
☐	☐
☐	☐

B. *Work in a group. Share and explain your choices. Which features does the group agree are important?*

C. *With your group, choose the same restaurant or movie to review. It should be one that all group members know. Choose three or four features from your list in Exercise A to include in your review.*

D. *On your own, write a review that follows this pattern:*

- A brief introduction of the restaurant or movie
- Your experiences at the restaurant, or your opinion of the movie
- Your recommendation to others

E. *Read your review aloud to your group. Discuss the similarities and differences in the reviews and your opinions.*

Further Practice

Project Idea

- Combine your group's reviews into a booklet, and exchange your booklet with another group.
- Read the other group's booklet. Identify these features in the reviews:
  - descriptive adjectives
  - verb tenses
  - sections of the review
  - overall recommendations

Journal or Blog Topic *(See Part 1, Units 1 and 2.)*

- Start a class Review Blog, where students can post reviews of books, movies, restaurants, websites, etc.

Writing Task 2: Write a review of a product or service.

A. *Choose a product or service to review. You can choose a real product you have bought or a service you have experienced, or you can imagine one. Complete this information.*

Product or service: _____

Brief explanation: _____

_____

_____

_____

_____

_____

Was your experience positive or negative? _____

How many stars would you give it? (★= lowest rating, ★ ★ ★ ★ ★ = highest rating)

_____

B. *On a separate piece of paper, brainstorm adjectives and phrases to describe the product or service and your recommendation.*

C. *Write your review. Follow the guidelines on page 228. Use descriptive vocabulary and the correct verb tenses. Remember to include an overall recommendation at the end.*

D. *Work in a group. Take turns reading your reviews. Can the listeners guess your rating for the product or service?*

Check Your Writing

A. *Use this form to check your own reviews, or exchange reviews with another student and check each other's writing.*

Reviews Checklist

Review 1

1. The review identifies the name of the restaurant or title of the movie. ☐
2. The review describes the type of restaurant / movie. ☐
3. The review describes the writer's personal experience. ☐
4. The writer makes an overall recommendation about the restaurant / movie. ☐
5. The writer used the appropriate verb tenses for different parts of a review. ☐
6. The writer used correct spelling and punctuation. ☐
7. What changes do you suggest to improve the review?

_____

_____

_____

Review 2

1. The review identifies the product or service. ☐
2. The review describes the product or business and what it does / offers. ☐
3. The review describes the writer's personal experience. ☐
4. The writer makes an overall recommendation about the product or service. ☐
5. The writer uses the appropriate verb tenses for different parts of a review. ☐
6. The writer uses correct spelling and punctuation. ☐
7. What changes do you suggest to improve the review?

_____

_____

_____

B. *Make changes to improve your reviews. Remember to check your writing for grammar, spelling, and punctuation errors.*

Current Events

People read, watch, or listen to the news to get information about current events—things that are happening in their local communities or the world right now. Current events may be news stories about the weather, sports, new movies, social or political situations, or opinions.

In addition to national and local (city) news, smaller communities such as schools, clubs, and companies often publish weekly or monthly newsletters or newspapers in order to keep their members updated on current events.

In this unit, you will practice writing a current events article that could become part of a class newsletter or school newspaper.

Writing about current events in English can help you . . .

- build vocabulary.
- improve writing skills and fluency.
- learn about your community.

Warm Up

A. *Look at these types of current events sources. Check (✓) the ones you use to read the news and write their titles. Add any other sources you use.*

Titles

☐ Local newspaper   _____

☐ National newspaper   _____

☐ News website   _____

☐ School or university newspaper   _____

☐ Company or organization newsletter _____

☐ Magazine   _____

☐ Other sources   _____

B. *Compare lists with another student. Do you use any of the same news sources? Discuss these questions:*

- Why do you choose those news sources? What do you like about them? What do you dislike?

- What types of news stories interest you the most?

C. *Take a class poll to find out the most popular news sources.*

CHARACTERISTICS OF NEWS ARTICLES

A news article is a special type of writing. It has a different format and style from other types of writing. This is mainly to help news publications fit a lot of information into a limited amount of space.

Format

As you have probably noticed, most newspaper and magazine articles are formatted with a headline (title) at the top. Then under the headline are columns with short paragraphs. This makes it easier and quicker to read.

Look at the sample article. Are newspapers in your culture formatted the same way?

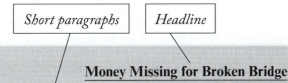

Short paragraphs   *Headline*

Money Missing for Broken Bridge

How much money does it take to repair an old bridge? According to the town council, money was approved for repairs to the Stone Park Bridge. Now, however, that money has disappeared because of a computer error.

Last year, the town applied for a special grant from the Department of Public Works (DPW) to repair the Stone Park Bridge. The DPW sent a letter saying the town had won the grant and would receive the money. Now, months later, no money has arrived, and the DPW says it has no record of awarding the money for the bridge repair. Town council members were outraged and sent a copy of the award letter to the DPW.

A DPW supervisor, Bill Vosofsky, responded immediately. He apologized to the town and said, "The mistake is ours. The money for the bridge is on the way." However, council members have doubts about how fast the money will arrive. The DPW has already spent its yearly budget. Council members are wondering where the DPW will find the money so it can fix the bridge before the winter.

The Stone Park Bridge was built fifty years ago. Its rustic design of wood and steel fit in with the peaceful wooded setting. Over the years, rain and snow have damaged the bridge. The bridge is on the path used by the many bikers and walkers who go to the park for exercise and meditation. One biker said, "If we don't repair the bridge, it will be a big loss. I will really miss riding in one of the most scenic areas of the park."

2 columns

Headlines

The headline or title of a news article is written to grab the attention of the reader. It also tells the reader what to expect in the article. Writers use special techniques to create interesting, powerful headlines.

Guidelines for Writing Headlines

A good headline . . .

- grabs the reader's attention

- captures the main idea of the news story

- is simple, short, and easy to read

- usually uses verbs in the simple present

- omits (leaves out) the verb *be* and less important words like articles and auxiliary verbs

Omitting Unnecessary Words

One common feature of headlines is omitting words such as the verb *be*, articles like *a*, *an*, and *the*, and auxiliary verbs.

Work with another student. Look at the examples. Discuss these questions:

- What do you notice about the verb tense in example 1?
- Which words are omitted in each example?

Examples:

1. *The students went to the new zoo.*

Students Go to New Zoo

2. *Tickets are now available for the town carnival.*

Tickets Available for Town Carnival

EXERCISE 1

A. ***Work in a group. Look at the headlines and try to guess the omitted words. Write the full sentence below each headline.***

1. **Titans Win Championship: Defeat Tigers 78–64**

   _____

2. **Townspeople Protest Approval of New Mall**

   _____

3. _____ **Massive Snowstorm Closes City Offices** _____

_____

4. _____ **New Bike Path: Cyclists' Safety Important Concern** _____

_____

5. _____ **New Professor Joins English Faculty** _____

_____

6. _____ **Surprisingly Low Attendance at Free Concert** _____

_____

B. *Work with another student. Read each headline in Exercise A. Discuss these questions:*

- What do you think the article will be about?
- Does the headline grab your attention? Why or why not?

EXERCISE 2

Work with another student. Create headlines for these sentences. Remember to use present tense verbs and omit unnecessary words.

1. A heavy rainfall caused the river to overflow.

_____

2. The city council completed a study about the increasing number of car accidents.

_____

3. The museum's new sculpture garden has opened.

_____

4. A local college student participated in a summer internship program and learned about marketing.

_____

5. The fitness center is hosting an opening day celebration for the public.

_____

Wh-Questions

Newspapers want readers to get information quickly and easily. To do this in an article, current events writers answer the information questions beginning with *Wh-* words, *Who*, *What*, *When*, *Where*, and *Why*, as well as *How*. For example, . . .

- *Who* was involved in the story?
- *What* is the story about?
- *Where* did the events take place?
- *When* did the events take place?
- *Why* did it happen?
- *How* did it happen?

EXERCISE 3

A. **Work with another student. Read the headline of the article from a university newspaper. Write the full sentence below.**

International Celebration Highlight of Term

By Lino Villamati and Ting Chen

_____

B. **What kind of information (who, what, where, when, why, how) do you think the article will include? Write your ideas. Then compare answers with a partner.**

Who: _____

What: _____

Where: _____

When: _____

Why: _____

How: _____

"Bravo, bravo," cheered the students. Then more laughter, thunderous applause, and music from around the world filled the Trent Hall auditorium last Friday for the International Culture Celebration.

The last days of school are usually devoted to intense studying and exams, and the same is true for our international students. However, on this day, after exams, the whole school was released from afternoon classes to participate in this much anticipated end-of-term event. The celebration included a presentation of the cultures, talents, and achievements of the many international students at the university.

The celebration included more than ten different presentations, including speeches, salsa dancers, saxophone players, readings of poems and essays, and much more.

One of the highlights was from Michael Park. Michael is from Korea and he wanted to share his national sport, tae kwon do.

He began with a short presentation which explained the philosophy and history of the sport. Michael spoke confidently and clearly.

Then, he gave a demonstration of some of the moves and ended it when he split five wooden boards with a powerful kick. Students gasped when they heard the crack of the wood. His classmates were aware he had an interest in the sport, but had no idea that he is considered a master teacher as well.

Julia Chaves from Brazil, said, "It was amazing!"

A student from Korea, Woo-Sik Yoo, said, "I'm so proud of my country. Tae kwon do is a great sport."

Another highlight of the celebration was a guitar performance by Gonzalo Hernandez from Brazil, who sang a song he wrote in English.

Audience members were captivated by the music. "The sound was just beautiful," said student Anna Kostadinow. "It was so soft and calming."

The final and most colorful event of the celebration was the international fashion show. Students volunteered to wear traditional costumes from their countries as a festive way to end their day of sharing their customs, special gifts, and language learning successes.

D. *Write the answers to the Wh- questions. Underline the sentences in the article that give the answers.*

1. Who was involved in the story? _____

2. What was the event? What happened? _____

3. Where did it take place? _____

4. When did it take place? _____

5. Why? _____

6. How? _____

E. *Compare answers in Exercise D with a partner. Discuss where you found the information in the article.*

Hooks and Lead-ins

In addition to headlines, news articles use hooks—sometimes called "lead-ins"—to grab the reader's attention in the first paragraph.

The following are types of hooks commonly used in current events articles. All the examples show how the different types of hooks could be used for an article about a student who is accepted into a university's MBA (Master's of Business Administration) program.

Questions

An interesting question that gets the reader thinking can work as a good hook.

Examples:

What do you need to do to get into a business administration program?

How many students do you think apply to MBA programs each year?

Surprising Facts or Statistics

Current events writers often get readers' attention by citing interesting facts or numerical statistics.

Examples:

Only 23 percent of all applicants are accepted into the university's business administration program annually.

Workers can greatly increase their salaries if they have an MBA.

Quotes and Sayings

A quote from someone involved with the story or a popular saying is an effective way to interest the reader.

Examples:

"This is a dream come true," said Salih upon learning that he had been accepted into an MBA program.

"Success is a journey, not a destination."
       —Arthur Ashe, champion tennis player

Anecdotes

An anecdote is an interesting short story or narration that illustrates or exemplifies the current event.

Example:

He had been anxiously waiting for weeks when one day the letter arrived from the university. He wanted to tear open the envelope, but he was afraid of what he might find. He paused and thought about how his future was in his hands. He carefully opened the envelope, unfolded the letter, and read it. Slowly, Salih smiled. Finally, he was on his way to getting his degree in business administration. His path to this goal had been long and difficult.

Salih's story is a familiar one. Every year hundreds of students apply to the university's business administration program, but fewer than 100 are admitted . . .

Note: See Part 3, Unit 6 for more about writing hooks.

EXERCISE 4

A. *Read the sentence (from the news article "International Celebration Highlight of Term"). What type of hook is it?*

   "Bravo, bravo," cheered the students.

B. *Work with another student. Read the "International Celebration" article on page 245 again. Write new types of hooks to begin the article.*

   1. A question:

   _____

   2. A surprising fact or statistic (the number of people who attended the celebration was 175):

   _____

   3. An anecdote:

   _____

   _____

   _____

   _____

   _____

C. *Share your new hooks with the class.*

Adding Details

The right details can bring news stories to life and add interest for the reader. Writers do this by describing the sights, sounds, or feelings of a current event. Details can include descriptions of people, places, or things, or quotations from people involved in the story.

> **Note:** Words that describe sounds, sights, and feelings are called sensory details. Use a dictionary to find words that describe the senses: sight, sound, touch, taste, and smell. Descriptive words can be nouns, adjectives, verbs, or adverbs.

Describing Sights

Describing people, places, and things helps the reader "see" the environment.

> ***Examples:***
> The _tired, sagging_ building needs many repairs.
> The _colorful tents and bright lights_ mean the carnival is in town.

Describing Sounds

Notice the special vocabulary used to describe sounds.

> ***Examples:***
> The music was _low and haunting_.
> The fans' _excited cheers_ could be heard for miles.
> The fire _roared_ as the building burned.

Describing Feelings

Words and quotations that describe feelings or a mood help the reader understand people's attitudes and emotions about an event or situation.

> ***Examples:***
> The ticket holders _looked thrilled_, although they had been waiting in line for hours to see the concert.
> One concert-goer said, "_I can't believe I'm really here. I want to scream!_"
> The manager _looked upset_ and refused to speak to reporters.

A. *Work with another student. Look at the examples from the article on page 245. Which aspects of the event do the examples describe? Write **sounds, sights, or feelings.** (You may write more than one.)*

1. "Bravo, bravo," cheered the students. Then more laughter, thunderous applause, and music from around the world . . .

_____

2. . . . the whole school was released from afternoon classes to participate in this much anticipated end-of-term event.

_____

3. . . . when he split five wooden boards with a powerful kick.

_____

4. Students gasped when they heard the crack of the wood.

_____

5. One student from Korea, Woo-Sik Yoo, said, "I'm so proud of my country. . . ."

_____

6. The final and most colorful event of the celebration was the international fashion show.

_____

B. *Work with your partner. Circle more examples of sounds, sights, and feelings in the article. Then compare them with another pair.*

A. *Work in a group. Choose a recent important event from the local, national, or international news. Discuss these questions:*

- What sights do you think people were able to see at the event?
- What kinds of sounds do you think they heard?
- What feelings do you imagine people had about the event?

(continued)

Use the chart to take notes on the group's ideas.

Sights	Sounds	Feelings

B. *On your own, write five sentences to describe the details of the event. Include descriptions of the sights, sounds, and feelings.*

Event: _____

1. _____

2. _____

3. _____

4. _____

5. _____

C. *Read your sentences aloud to the class. Can they guess the event?*

Writing Quotations

When you write down the exact words someone says, you must use quotation marks. Adding quotations is another way to add details and depth to the story. When you write quotations, you need to use special punctuation.

Guidelines for Writing Quotations

- Use quotation marks at the start and end of the exact words used by the speaker. At the end, place periods or commas inside the quotation marks.

    "I'm so proud of my country. Tae kwon do is a great sport."

- Use a comma after a verb that introduces the quotation and a capital letter for the first word of the quotation.

    Julia Chaves from Brazil said, "It was amazing!"

- If the sentence starts with the quotation, add a comma at the end of the last word and then a quotation mark and continue with the rest of the sentence.

    "Bravo, bravo," cheered the students.

- Put question marks or exclamation points inside the quotation marks if they are part of the exact words of the speaker.

    Julia Chaves from Brazil said, "It was amazing!"

- Put closing quotation marks around the last word of the speaker, not before.

Incorrect:

One student from Korea, Woo-Sik Yoo, said, "I'm so proud of my country.✗ ✗Tae kwon do is a great sport."

Correct:

One student from Korea, Woo-Sik Yoo, said, "I'm so proud of my country. Tae kwon do is a great sport."

- In a two-sentence quote, it's possible to place the subject between the sentences. Put quotation marks at the beginning and end of both sentences. Put a comma at the end of the first sentence.

    "The sound was just beautiful," said student Anna Kostadinow. "It was so soft and calming."

The quotations below contain no punctuation. Rewrite them with correct punctuation. Follow the guidelines for writing quotations.

1. I used to walk over that bridge every day said resident Karen Marston

   _____

   _____

2. The supervisor said the town will get the money for the bridge we will correct this mistake immediately

   _____

   _____

3. I can't believe I finally did it said Salih It's a great feeling

   _____

   _____

4. I am so happy for you said Salih's teacher

   _____

   _____

5. I've never seen so much rain in all of my life said Jenna Adams

   _____

   _____

6. The first floor of the art building was completely flooded said art major Mike Yamano We had to get out quickly

   _____

   _____

7. When you have a win like this, you know that your players are really working as a team said coach Mathers

   _____

   _____

8. One of the players senior Jim Armenti said It helps to have a great coach

   _____

   _____

WRITING TASK

Write a current events article that could appear in a school newspaper.

A. *Work in a group. Use the list below to brainstorm recent news or events at your school or in your city. Take notes on your group's ideas.*

a sporting event

_____

a musical or theater performance

_____

a new movie, CD, or book

_____

a speech, lecture, or presentation

_____

a political election

_____

information about public transportation

_____

changes to student services at school; for example, new gym hours, cafeteria closings, etc.

_____

unusual weather

_____

an art exhibit

_____

a new restaurant or shop

_____

a person's accomplishments; for example, a student or teacher

_____

B. *On your own, choose an event you know about from the list in Exercise A. (Or choose a different event.)*

Remember

Consider your audience: Your article should be about an event that is interesting and relevant to the reader.

C. *What information do you know about the story? Ask yourself the Wh- questions. What information do you still need in order to write your article?*

1. *Who* was involved in the story/event?

   _____

2. *What* happened?

   _____

3. *Where* did it take place?

   _____

(continued)

4. *When* did it take place?

_____

5. *Why?*

_____

6. *How?*

_____

Note: If you need more information, you can interview a person (or people) involved in the event. You can do this by email, telephone, or in person.

Tips for interviewing:
- Research your topic and plan ahead.
- Decide what questions you will ask and write them down.
- Consider recording the interview to help you remember the details and write the quotations. (Be sure to ask for the interviewee's permission before recording.)
- Think about how you will greet your interviewee and make him or her feel comfortable (small talk, etc.).
- Think about how you will end the interview (thanking the interviewee for his or her time and the information, etc.).

D. **Write details and quotations that include the sounds, sights, and feelings of the story. Use a separate piece of paper if you need more space.**

	Sights	**Sounds**	**Feelings**
Details			
Quotations			

E. **On a separate piece of paper, write a headline and a hook for your article.**

Remember

- The headline should be short and simple, and capture the main idea of the story or event.
- The hook can be an anecdote, a question, a surprising fact or statistic, or a quotation.

F. **Complete your news article. Include details, quotations, and try to answer all of the Wh- questions.**

Check Your Writing

A. *Use this form to check your own article, or exchange articles with another student and check each other's writing.*

Current Events Article Checklist

1. Is the article relevant and interesting? Why or why not?

_____

2. Does the headline express the main idea of the story or event?

_____

3. What kind of hook is used?

_____

4. What details and quotations describe the sounds, sights, and feelings of the event?

_____

_____

_____

5. Is the article easy to follow? Are any sections or sentences confusing? If so, which ones?

_____

6. What suggestions do you have to improve the article?

_____

_____

_____

B. *Make changes to improve your article. Remember to check your writing for grammar, spelling, and punctuation errors.*

Further Practice

Journal or Blog Topic *(See Part 1, Units 1 and 2.)*
- Write an article about one of the topics you did NOT use for the Writing Task.

Project Idea
- Make a class or school newspaper. Collect news articles from students in your class or school and divide them by topic and section (News, Weather, Events, Reviews, etc.).
- Add photos or drawings and make a copy for every student in the class.

UNIT 5

College Application Essays

College application essays are often required for admission to colleges or universities. Every year, schools receive thousands of applications from students with excellent test scores and grades. The essay helps admissions officers decide which students to accept into their schools. Sometimes the application essay is called a "personal statement," especially on applications for graduate schools. The essay may become the deciding factor in whether a student is accepted to a school or not.

In this unit, you will gather ideas for, prepare, and write your own college application essay, including:

- Creating a timeline of important events in your life
- Brainstorming your achievements, skills, and influences
- Choosing a topic
- Planning your essay

Warm Up

A. *Work in a group. Discuss these questions:*

- Do the words "college" and "university" mean the same thing in your culture? What types and levels of colleges and universities are there in your culture?
- How are students usually admitted to colleges or universities (for example, a test, an interview, etc.)?
- What characteristics, skills, and experiences are important for students to have in order to enter university?

B. *Discuss your answers with the class.*

EXTRAORDINARY YOU

Schools want to know who you are and what makes you special. They also want to see how well you can organize and express your ideas in writing. The application essay gives you an opportunity to show schools both.

Depending on the school, the application essay may have different topics to choose from. Topics generally require you to write about yourself and your experience, ideas, and opinions.

Before you choose your application essay topic, you will need to take some time to think about what makes you unique. Think about all of your experiences and accomplishments, your high and low moments, and your hobbies, interests, and influences.

Life Events

Your essay needs to be specific to your life events and the impact these events have made on you. These events may or may not be positive. The important thing is how the experience has shaped who you are. One way to begin organizing your ideas is to create a timeline. Begin with the year you were born. Continue adding important events and the year they happened.

EXERCISE 1

A. *Read the sample timeline of important events in a student's life. Then create a timeline of your own life on a separate piece of paper.*

1993	born in New York City, lived in apartment building with people from all over the world
1998	started school
2000	moved to small town, surrounded by nature
2003	went to another country for the first time—Mexico
2006	joined youth group in another town and made new friends
2007	first year of high school; started playing football
2008	did school play <u>Bye, Bye, Birdie</u>, joined varsity football team
2009	got first job at camp
2010	graduated from high school

B. *Compare your timeline with another student. Ask questions about each other's experiences. Explain why the events are important.*

Skills and Strengths

Your essay needs to highlight your skills and strengths in order to show what is special about you. These skills and strengths are your achievements and abilities, like speaking another language, academic awards, part-time jobs, or volunteer experience. Brainstorming skills and strengths will give you ideas for things you can emphasize in your essay.

EXERCISE 2

A. *Complete the chart with information about your skills and strengths.*

Education	**Awards**
Jobs	**Volunteer Work**
Travel	**Languages**
Membership in Clubs/Organizations	**Hobbies**
Sports	**Other Skills and Strengths**
Personal Characteristics	

B. *Compare charts with another student. Ask questions about each other's skills and strengths. Which ones do you think would be important to include in an application essay?*

Influences

Your essay may focus on someone or something that has influenced you—an experience or a person that has changed you in some way, either by teaching you something important, broadening your viewpoint, or changing your way of thinking or doing things.

A person who has influenced you may be a family member, a friend, a teacher, or a famous person. Other types of influences include travel, local or world events, classes you have taken, music, books, movies, or artwork.

EXERCISE 3

A. On a separate piece of paper, write your answers to these questions:

- Who is someone you know that has influenced you or your life? In what way has this person changed you?

- What famous person has influenced you the most? How?

- What is the best book you have ever read? How did it affect you or your way of thinking?

- What is the best movie you have ever seen? How did it affect you or your way of thinking?

- In your opinion, what has been the most important world event (past or present, positive or negative)? How did it affect you or your way of thinking?

- What else has influenced you that is not listed above? How has it changed you?

B. Compare answers with another student. How are your influences the same? How are they different?

ESSAY FORMAT AND STRUCTURE

Essays may be part of an online form, or on a separate form that you submit by email or mail.

Schools may or may not provide instructions about the length and format of the essay. The length can range from 250 words to as many as 900 words. If a word limit is given, it is very important to stay within that limit. If a limit is not given, generally, two pages of double-spaced text is an acceptable length.

The application essay follows a formal essay format with an introduction, body paragraphs, and a conclusion.

- The **introduction** includes your topic and main idea. For example, it introduces a person or an experience that has influenced you and gives a general description of how.

- The **body paragraphs** include details, explanations, and examples that support your main idea. For example, each paragraph might list a way in which the person or experience influenced you, and tells a story or gives examples and details to show how.

> **Note:** In an essay, each body paragraph develops one subtopic that supports the main idea of the essay. (See Part 3, Unit 1 for more on essay structure.)

- The **conclusion** sums up your main points and why the school you are applying to is the right school for you.

EXERCISE 4

A. *Work with another student. Read the sentences. What part of the essay are they from? Write I for introduction, B for body paragraphs, or C for conclusion. (More than one answer may be possible for some sentences.)*

_____ 1. In addition to sports, I also had an interest in acting and singing.

_____ 2. As a young child, I lived in an apartment in New York City.

_____ 3. My high school classmates were not as accepting or open-minded as my new friends.

_____ 4. It wasn't until I was a teenager that I rediscovered my interest in people with different backgrounds.

_____ 5. These experiences gave me an appreciation for people who were different from me.

_____ 6. At this university, I will not be the type of student who just sits in a dorm room all semester.

_____ 7. Not long after my eighth birthday, my family moved to a small town.

_____ 8. Sometimes taking a chance in life can make all the difference.

B. *Compare answers with another student. To check your answers, find the sentences in the essay in Exercise 9 on pages 265–266.*

APPLICATION ESSAY TOPICS

The application form—whether online or on paper— includes instructions for writing the essay and a list of essay questions or topics. Students choose one question or topic and write about it.

Questions and topics usually focus on . . .

- a person or an experience that has influenced you.

- something that is special about you and your experience, and how that would benefit the school or contribute to the student population.

- something about the school you are applying to and why you want to go there.

Note: Some schools are known for their creative or unusual essay questions, or even for asking students to submit video applications. If you are especially creative, answering this type of question or making a video may be the way you can become memorable in the eyes of the admissions officers.

EXERCISE 5

A. *Read the sample essay topics with a partner. Write some ideas for what you would write about for each one. Use your timeline, skills and strengths chart, and ideas from the discussion questions in Exercise 3 to help you.*

Topic A
The university community is a mixture of people from different backgrounds and experiences. How would you share your perspective with others at the university as a result of your own experiences, traits, and cultural background?

_____

_____

_____

Topic B
Describe someone who has influenced you and how.

_____

_____

_____

Topic C
Write about an accomplishment or risk you have taken and its effects on you.

_____

_____

_____

(continued)

Topic D

Describe how a movie, book, piece of music, or other creative work has influenced you.

_____

_____

_____

    B.   *Talk with a partner. Which essay topic would you choose? Why?*

EXERCISE 6

    A.   *Read the brainstorm from a student who chose this topic:* **Write about an accomplishment or risk you have taken and its effects on you.**

<u>Childhood</u>
- born in New York City
- lived in an apartment building with people from all over the world
- ~~ate different kinds of food from different cultures~~
- moved to a small town
- different experience, quieter, surrounded by nature
- outdoor activities like playing in the snow and swimming
- ~~played on a soccer team~~
- became involved in special club called Leaders
- met new people
- had to develop leadership skills

<u>High school years</u>
- ~~took a trip to Mexico~~
- new classmates; different from other people I knew
- got on the football team, new experience, demanding, hard
- liked theater, did the school play
- football friends against my doing the play, did it anyway
- was accepted for doing something unusual for a football player
- taking chances is important for development and social involvement

B. *Look at the student's brainstorm in Exercise A. Notice the details he chose to cross out. Why do you think he chose not to include them?*

C. *Work with another student. Discuss which points in the brainstorm colleges/universities would be most interested in knowing about the student.*

EXERCISE 7

A. *Choose one of the topics from Exercise 5 to write about. Do a brainstorm about the topic on the paper below.*

Note: When you brainstorm, the point is to list as many ideas as you can. Work quickly and list all your ideas. Do not stop to think about or choose the ones you like the best. You can do that after you complete the brainstorm.

B. *Compare your brainstorm with another student. Ask questions to find out more information. Add more details to your brainstorm if you can.*

C. *Review your brainstorm and decide which details are the most important for your topic. Cross out any details that are not directly related to your topic.*

A. *Look at how the student organized his brainstorm from Exercise 6 into the essay format.*

Introduction – Childhood
- born in New York City
- lived in an apartment building with people from all over the world

Body Paragraphs – Experiences
Moved to a small town
- different experience, quieter, nature
- outdoor activities like playing in the snow and swimming

Became involved in special club called Teen Leaders
- met new people
- had to develop leadership skills

High school years
- new classmates; different from other people I knew
- got on the football team, new experience, demanding, hard
- liked theater, did the school play
- football friends against my doing the play, did it anyway
- was accepted for doing something unusual for a football player

Conclusion – Taking Risks Important
- taking chances is important for development and social involvement
- this university will make me leave my comfort zone

B. *Organize the information from your brainstorm in Exercise 7C into the essay structure. Make notes on what to include in the introduction, the body, and the conclusion. Use the example in Exercise A to help you.*

A. Read the essay the student wrote using the notes in Exercise 8.

As a young child, I lived in an apartment in New York City. At that time, I did not fully realize the importance of the cultural diversity that I was exposed to every day. Every time I walked into my apartment building, the Latino doorman greeted me. In the building, I could hear the sounds of many different languages all at once, whether it was the Puerto Rican family down the hall, or the Chinese family on the seventh floor. At school, I had friends from many different cultures. These experiences gave me an appreciation for people who were different from me, and a desire for new and interesting experiences.

Not long after my eighth birthday, my family moved to a small town. The environment was a big change from the city. It was a lot quieter, and I noticed the lack of cultural variety. As a youth, it did not bother me much. To me, the hot summers down at the lake and riding my bike were the most important parts of life.

It wasn't until I was a teenager that I rediscovered my interest in people with different backgrounds. A neighbor asked me if I wanted to join a community service group called Teen Leaders, so I did. Little did I know that this would be one of the most important experiences of my life. The people I met there were all similar to me. They were also interested in meeting people from various cultural backgrounds. A few of the people I met there would become some of my closest friends.

My high school classmates were not as accepting or open-minded as my new friends in my Teen Leaders group. I played for the football team, and there were certain ways all the football players were "supposed to" act. I didn't exactly fit.

In addition to sports, I also had an interest in acting and singing. Trying out for the school play my sophomore year was not considered a smart choice by my football teammates. In fact, they made fun of me. However, when I got the lead role in the musical play *Bye, Bye Birdie,* I stuck with it despite their constant teasing.

(continued)

The opening night of the show arrived. When the first song ended, I heard a loud roar of shouting and cheers from one section of the audience. It was my football teammates. I thought they had come to make fun of me. After the show ended, I was nervous about seeing them. When I walked out those doors, I was shocked by my friends' reactions. They told me my performance was great. I had mistaken their loud cheers for teasing, but in fact, they were cheers of enthusiasm.

Sometimes taking a chance in life can make all the difference. Leaving my comfort zone was an important step in my development. Now I have the ability to enter new situations confidently. At this university, I will not be the type of student who just sits in a dorm room all semester. I will be the one encouraging others to get involved in university activities and in the community. In conclusion, I hope other students will feel the same acceptance and pride that I experienced.

B. *Work with another student. Discuss these questions:*

- How does the student begin his essay?

- What is the main idea of the essay?

- What kinds of influences, experiences, and skills does the student include?

- List some of the specific examples the student included here:

  _____

  _____

  _____

  _____

  _____

- How would you describe this student?

- Do you think university admissions officers will have a clear understanding of this student's character? Why or why not?

Application Essay Do's and Don'ts

Application officers are looking for your ability to compose a well-written essay. Here are some tips for writing your application essay:

Do

- Give yourself plenty of time to plan and write your essay. Don't leave it for the last minute. You should allow yourself three to four weeks to complete your essay.

- Look at the question carefully and follow the directions. Talk about the topic choices with a teacher, friend, or family member to help you decide which topic shows the best of you!

- Write a good beginning to capture the reader's interest. You don't want to begin by writing about how much you want to go to a particular school. Instead, start by showing the reader something special about you or your experience.

- Be sure to proofread your essay. An essay full of errors is not acceptable. It's a good idea to have someone else check your essay for errors before you send it in.

Don't

- Write an essay that is full of generalizations. Include enough details, explanations, and specific examples to show your unique experiences, strengths, and skills.

- Go over the word limit or page limit. Your essay will not be seriously considered if you have not followed the directions.

- Be repetitive.

WRITING TASK

Write your own college application essay.

A. **Review the materials you have created in preparation for writing a college application essay.**

- Your timeline of important life events
- Your skills and strengths chart on page 258
- Your answers to the questions about influences in Exercise 3

B. *Choose your essay topic. Choose topic A, B, C, or D from Exercise 5. (You can choose the same topic you wrote your brainstorm for in Exercise 7, or you can choose a different topic.)*

If you chose a different topic. . .

- write a brainstorm about the topic.
- select what to include.
- organize your brainstorm into the essay structure (introduction, body, conclusion).

C. *Use your brainstorm to write the first draft of your application essay. Your essay should be between 400 and 500 words.*

Check Your Writing

A. *Use this form to check your own essay, or exchange essays with another student and check each other's writing.*

Application Essay Checklist

1. The essay includes information about . . .
   - experiences. ☐
   - skills and strengths. ☐
   - influences. ☐

2. The essay is the correct length. ☐

3. The essay follows the correct essay structure (introduction, body paragraphs, conclusion). ☐

4. The introduction includes the topic and the main idea. ☐

5. The body paragraphs include details and examples to support the main idea. ☐

6. The conclusion gives a summary of the main idea. ☐

7. What suggestions do you have to improve the essay?

   _____

   _____

   _____

   _____

B. *Make changes to improve your essay. Remember to check your writing for grammar, spelling, and punctuation errors.*

APPENDIX

Frequently Used Words in English

This list was compiled from the Pearson International Corpus of Academic English. It contains the top 3,000 words in the corpus ranked by raw frequency. The Pearson International Corpus of Academic English, Version 1.2010 was developed and is owned by Pearson Language Tests, London, UK, a division of Edexcel Ltd (http://www.pearsonpte.com/).

a	adapt	alien	apparent	assessment	band
abandon	adaptation	alike	apparently	asset	bank
ability	add	alive	appeal	assign	bar
able	addition	all	appear	assignment	barrier
about	additional	allocate	appearance	assist	base
above	address	allow	applicable	assistance	basic
abroad	adequate	ally	applicant	assistant	basically
absence	adequately	almost	application	associate	basis
absent	adjacent	alone	apply	association	battle
absolute	adjust	along	appoint	assume	be
absolutely	adjustment	alongside	appointment	assumption	bear
absorb	administer	already	appreciate	assure	beat
abstract	administration	also	appreciation	at	beautiful
abuse	administrative	alter	approach	atmosphere	beauty
academic	admission	alternative	appropriate	atom	because
accelerate	admit	alternatively	appropriately	attach	become
accept	adopt	although	approval	attachment	bed
acceptable	adoption	altogether	approve	attack	before
acceptance	adult	always	approximately	attain	begin
access	advance	amazing	arbitrary	attempt	beginning
accessible	advanced	ambiguity	architecture	attend	behalf
accident	advantage	ambiguous	area	attention	behave
accommodate	advertising	among	arena	attitude	behavior
accommodation	advice	amongst	argue	attract	behind
accompany	advise	amount	argument	attraction	being
accomplish	advocate	an	arise	attractive	belief
accord	aesthetic	analogy	arm	attribute	believe
accordance	affair	analysis	army	audience	belong
accordingly	affect	analyst	around	author	below
account	afford	analytical	arrange	authority	beneficial
accumulate	afraid	analyze	arrangement	automatic	benefit
accuracy	after	ancient	array	automatically	besides
accurate	afternoon	and	arrest	autonomous	between
accurately	again	anger	arrival	autonomy	beyond
accuse	against	angle	arrive	availability	bias
achieve	age	angry	art	available	big
achievement	agency	animal	article	average	bill
acid	agenda	announce	articulate	avoid	billion
acknowledge	agent	annual	artificial	award	binary
acquire	aggressive	another	artist	aware	bind
acquisition	ago	answer	artistic	awareness	biological
across	agree	anticipate	as	away	biology
act	agreement	anxiety	aside	baby	bird
action	agricultural	any	ask	back	birth
active	ahead	anybody	aspect	background	bit
actively	aid	anyone	aspiration	bad	black
activity	aim	anything	assemble	bag	blame
actor	air	anyway	assert	balance	blind
actual	albeit	anywhere	assertion	ball	block
actually	alcohol	apart	assess	ban	blood

blow
blue
board
body
bond
bone
book
border
borrow
both
bottom
boundary
box
boy
brain
branch
brand
break
breakdown
bridge
brief
briefly
bright
brilliant
bring
broad
broaden
broadly
brother
budget
build
building
burden
burn
bus
business
busy
but
buy
by
calculate
calculation
call
camera
camp
campaign
campus
can
cancer
candidate
capability
capable
capacity
capital
capitalism
capitalist
capture
car
carbon
card
care
career
careful
carefully
carry

case
cash
cast
catch
category
cause
caution
cease
celebrate
celebrity
cell
cent
center
central
centre
century
ceremony
certain
certainly
chain
chair
challenge
chance
change
channel
chapter
character
characteristic
characterize
charge
chart
cheap
check
chemical
chemistry
chief
child
childhood
choice
choose
church
circle
circuit
circumstance
cite
citizen
city
civil
claim
clarify
clarity
class
classic
classical
classification
classify
classroom
clean
clear
clearly
client
climate
clinical
close
closed

closely
closer
clothes
clothing
cloud
club
clue
cluster
coast
code
coffee
cognitive
coherent
coin
coincide
cold
collaboration
collapse
colleague
collect
collection
collective
college
color
column
com
combat
combination
combine
combined
come
comfort
comfortable
command
comment
commentary
commentator
commercial
commission
commit
commitment
committee
commodity
common
commonly
communicate
communication
community
company
comparable
comparative
compare
comparison
compatible
compensate
compensation
compete
competence
competition
competitive
complain
complaint
complement
complete
completely

completion
complex
complexity
complicate
complicated
component
compose
composition
compound
comprehensive
comprise
compromise
computer
conceive
concentrate
concentration
concept
conception
conceptual
concern
concerned
conclude
conclusion
concrete
condition
conduct
conference
confidence
confident
configuration
confine
confirm
conflict
conform
confront
confuse
confusion
conjunction
connect
connection
conscious
consciousness
consensus
consent
consequence
consequently
conservative
consider
considerable
considerably
consideration
consist
consistency
consistent
consistently
constant
constantly
constituent
constitute
constrain
constraint
construct
construction
consult
consultation

consume
consumer
consumption
contact
contain
contemporary
content
contest
context
continually
continue
continued
continuity
continuous
contract
contradiction
contrary
contrast
contribute
contribution
control
controversial
controversy
convenient
convention
conventional
conversation
conversely
conversion
convert
convey
conviction
convince
cool
cooperation
coordinate
cope
copy
core
corner
corporate
corporation
correct
correctly
correlation
correspond
correspondence
corresponding
cost
could
council
counsel
count
counter
counterpart
country
couple
course
court
cover
coverage
create
creation
creative
creativity

credit
crime
criminal
crisis
criterion
critic
critical
critically
criticism
criticize
critique
crop
cross
crowd
crucial
cry
cultural
culture
curious
current
currently
curriculum
curve
custom
customer
cut
cycle
daily
damage
dance
danger
dangerous
dark
data
database
date
datum
daughter
day
dead
deal
death
debate
debt
decade
decide
decision
declare
decline
decrease
dedicate
deem
deep
deeply
defeat
defense
defend
define
definitely
definition
degree
delay
deliberately
deliver
delivery

demand	disagreement	during	empty	every	express
democracy	disappear	duty	enable	everybody	expression
democratic	disaster	dynamic	enact	everyday	extend
demonstrate	discipline	dynamics	encompass	everyone	extended
demonstration	discourse	each	encounter	everything	extension
denote	discover	ear	encourage	everywhere	extensive
density	discovery	earlier	end	evidence	extent
deny	discrete	early	endorse	evident	external
department	discrimination	earn	enemy	evil	extra
departure	discuss	earth	energy	evolution	extract
depend	discussion	ease	enforce	evolve	extraordinary
dependence	disease	easily	engage	exact	extreme
dependent	dismiss	eastern	engagement	exactly	extremely
depict	disorder	easy	engine	exam	eye
deposit	displace	echo	engineer	examination	face
depression	display	economic	engineering	examine	facilitate
depth	dispute	economics	enhance	example	facility
derive	dissolve	economy	enjoy	exceed	fact
describe	distance	edge	enormous	excellent	factor
description	distant	edit	enough	except	factory
deserve	distinct	edition	ensure	exception	faculty
design	distinction	editor	entail	exceptional	fail
designate	distinctive	educate	enter	excess	failure
desirable	distinguish	education	enterprise	excessive	fair
desire	distribute	educational	entertainment	exchange	fairly
despite	distribution	effect	enthusiasm	excite	faith
destination	district	effective	entire	exciting	fall
destroy	diverse	effectively	entirely	exclude	familiar
destruction	diversity	effectiveness	entitle	exclusion	family
detail	divide	efficiency	entity	exclusive	famous
detailed	division	efficient	entry	exclusively	fan
detect	divorce	effort	environment	excuse	fantastic
determination	do	eight	environmental	executive	fantasy
determine	doctor	either	episode	exemplify	far
develop	doctrine	elaborate	equal	exercise	farm
development	document	elect	equality	exert	farmer
device	dog	election	equally	exhibit	fascinating
devise	dollar	electric	equation	exhibition	fashion
devote	domain	electrical	equilibrium	exist	fast
diagram	domestic	electron	equip	existence	faster
dialogue	dominance	electronic	equipment	existing	fat
dictate	dominant	element	equivalent	expand	fate
die	dominate	eligible	era	expansion	father
diet	door	eliminate	error	expect	fault
differ	double	elite	escape	expectation	favor
difference	doubt	else	especially	expenditure	fear
different	down	elsewhere	essay	expense	feature
differential	dozen	email	essence	expensive	federal
differentiate	draft	embed	essential	experience	fee
differently	drama	embody	essentially	experienced	feed
difficult	dramatic	embrace	establish	experiment	feedback
difficulty	dramatically	emerge	established	experimental	feel
digital	draw	emergence	establishment	expert	feeling
dilemma	drawing	emergency	estate	expertise	fellow
dimension	dream	emission	estimate	explain	female
diminish	dress	emotion	ethic	explanation	feminist
dinner	drink	emotional	ethical	explicit	few
direct	drinking	emphasis	ethnic	explicitly	fiction
direction	drive	emphasize	evaluate	exploit	field
directly	driver	empirical	evaluation	exploitation	fifth
director	drop	employ	even	exploration	fifty
dirt	drug	employee	evening	explore	fight
disability	dry	employer	event	export	figure
disadvantage	due	employment	eventually	expose	file
disagree	duration		ever	exposure	fill

film
filter
final
finally
finance
financial
find
finding
fine
finger
finish
fire
firm
firmly
first
firstly
fish
fit
five
fix
flat
flexibility
flexible
flight
flood
floor
flow
fluid
fly
focus
folk
follow
following
food
foot
football
for
force
foreign
forest
forget
form
formal
formally
format
formation
former
formula
formulate
formulation
forth
forum
forward
foster
found
foundation
founder
four
fourth
fraction
fragment
frame
framework
free
freedom

freely
frequency
frequent
frequently
fresh
friend
friendly
friendship
from
front
fruit
fuel
fulfill
full
fully
fun
function
functional
fund
fundamental
fundamentally
funding
funny
further
furthermore
future
gain
game
gap
garden
gas
gather
gay
gender
general
generally
generate
generation
generic
genetic
genre
genuine
geographical
geography
gesture
get
giant
gift
girl
give
glass
global
go
goal
god
gold
good
govern
government
grade
gradually
graduate
grand
grant
graph

grasp
great
greatly
green
gross
ground
group
grow
growth
guarantee
guard
guess
guest
guidance
guide
guideline
guilty
guy
habit
hair
half
hall
hand
handle
hang
happen
happy
hard
hardly
harm
hate
have
he
head
health
healthy
hear
hearing
heart
heat
heavily
heavy
height
help
helpful
hence
her
here
hero
herself
hidden
hide
hierarchy
high
highlight
highly
him
himself
hint
hire
his
historian
historical
historically
history

hit
hold
hole
holiday
home
honest
hope
hopefully
horse
hospital
host
hot
hour
house
household
housing
how
however
huge
human
humanity
hundred
hurt
husband
hybrid
hypothesis
ice
idea
ideal
identical
identification
identify
identity
ideological
ideology
if
ignore
ill
illegal
illness
illustrate
illustration
image
imagination
imagine
immediate
immediately
impact
imperative
implement
implementation
implication
implicit
imply
import
importance
important
importantly
impose
impossible
impress
impression
impressive
improve
improvement

impulse
in
inability
inadequate
inappropriate
incentive
incident
include
inclusion
income
incorporate
increase
increasingly
indeed
independence
independent
independently
index
indicate
indication
indicator
indigenous
indirect
individual
individually
induce
industrial
industry
inequality
inevitable
inevitably
infant
influence
influential
inform
informal
information
infrastructure
inherent
inherit
initial
initially
initiate
initiative
injury
inner
innovation
innovative
input
inquiry
insert
inside
insight
insist
inspiration
inspire
instance
instead
institution
institutional
instruction
instrument
insurance
integral
integrate

integrated
integration
integrity
intellectual
intelligence
intend
intense
intensity
intensive
intent
intention
interact
interaction
interactive
interest
interested
interesting
interfere
intermediate
internal
international
interpret
interpretation
interrupt
interval
intervene
intervention
interview
intimate
into
introduce
introduction
invent
invest
investigate
investigation
investment
invite
invoke
involve
involvement
ion
iron
irrelevant
island
isolate
isolated
isolation
issue
it
item
its
itself
job
join
joint
joke
journal
journalist
journey
judge
judgment
jump
just
justice

justification	likelihood	map	mission	need	ocean
justify	likely	margin	mistake	negative	odd
keen	likewise	mark	mix	neglect	of
keep	limit	market	mixed	negotiate	off
key	limitation	marketing	mixture	negotiation	offer
kick	limited	marriage	mobile	neither	office
kid	line	marry	mobility	nervous	officer
kill	linear	mass	mode	net	official
kind	linguistic	massive	model	network	often
know	link	master	moderate	neutral	oil
knowledge	liquid	match	modern	never	okay
label	list	material	modest	nevertheless	old
labor	listen	mathematical	modification	new	on
laboratory	literally	matrix	modify	newly	once
lack	literary	matter	molecular	news	one
lady	literature	mature	molecule	newspaper	ongoing
land	little	maximum	moment	next	online
landscape	live	may	money	nice	only
language	living	maybe	monitor	night	onto
large	load	me	month	nine	open
largely	loan	meal	mood	nineteenth	opening
last	local	mean	moral	no	operate
late	locate	meaning	more	nobody	operation
later	location	meaningful	moreover	noise	operator
latter	lock	means	morning	none	opinion
laugh	log	measure	most	nonetheless	opponent
launch	logic	measurement	mostly	nor	opportunity
law	logical	mechanical	mother	norm	oppose
lawyer	long	mechanism	motion	normal	opposite
lay	longer	medical	motivate	normally	opposition
layer	look	medicine	motivation	north	optical
lead	loose	medium	motive	northern	option
leader	lose	meet	motor	not	or
leadership	loss	meeting	mount	notable	oral
learn	lot	member	mountain	notably	order
learning	love	membership	mouth	note	ordinary
least	low	memory	move	nothing	organ
leave	lower	mental	movement	notice	organic
lecture	machine	mention	movie	notion	organization
lecturer	magazine	mere	much	novel	organize
left	magnitude	merely	multiple	now	orient
leg	main	merge	multiply	nowhere	orientation
legacy	mainly	merit	murder	nuclear	origin
legal	mainstream	message	music	number	original
legislation	maintain	metal	musical	numerous	originally
legitimate	maintenance	metaphor	must	nurse	originate
leisure	major	method	mutual	object	other
lend	majority	methodology	my	objection	otherwise
length	make	middle	myself	objective	ought
less	maker	might	myth	obligation	our
lesser	making	migration	name	obscure	ourselves
lesson	male	mile	namely	observation	out
let	man	military	narrative	observe	outcome
letter	manage	million	narrow	observer	outline
level	management	mind	nation	obstacle	output
liberal	manager	mine	national	obtain	outside
liberty	manifest	minimal	native	obvious	outstanding
library	manifestation	minimum	natural	obviously	over
lie	manipulate	minister	naturally	occasion	overall
life	manipulation	minor	nature	occasional	overcome
lifestyle	manner	minority	near	occasionally	overlap
lifetime	manual	minute	nearly	occupation	overlook
lift	manufacture	mirror	necessarily	occupy	overseas
light	manufacturing	mislead	necessary	occur	overview
like	many	miss	necessity	occurrence	overwhelming

owe
own
owner
ownership
pace
pack
package
page
pain
paint
painting
pair
panel
paper
paradigm
paragraph
parallel
parameter
parent
park
part
partial
partially
participant
participate
participation
particle
particular
particularly
partly
partner
partnership
party
pass
passage
passion
passive
past
path
pathway
patient
pattern
pay
payment
peace
peak
peer
penalty
people
per
perceive
percent
percentage
perception
perfect
perfectly
perform
performance
perhaps
period
permanent
permission
permit
persist
person

personal
personality
personally
personnel
perspective
persuade
phase
phenomenon
philosopher
philosophical
philosophy
phone
photo
photograph
phrase
physical
physically
pick
picture
piece
pioneer
place
placement
plain
plan
plane
planet
planning
plant
plastic
plate
platform
play
player
please
pleasure
plenty
plot
plus
poem
poet
poetry
point
police
policy
political
politically
politician
politics
pollution
pool
poor
poorly
pop
popular
popularity
population
portion
portray
pose
position
positive
positively
possess
possession

possibility
possible
possibly
post
potential
potentially
pound
poverty
power
powerful
practical
practice
practitioner
praise
precede
precise
precisely
predict
prediction
predominantly
prefer
preference
preferred
prejudice
preliminary
premise
preparation
prepare
presence
present
presentation
preserve
president
press
pressure
presumably
pretend
pretty
prevail
prevent
previous
previously
price
pride
primarily
primary
prime
principal
principle
print
prior
priority
prison
private
privilege
prize
probability
probably
problem
problematic
procedure
proceed
proceeding
process
processing

produce
producer
product
production
productive
productivity
profession
professional
professor
profile
profit
profound
program
progress
progressive
prohibit
project
prominent
promise
promote
promotion
prompt
proof
proper
properly
property
proportion
proposal
propose
proposition
prospect
protect
protection
protest
proud
prove
provide
provider
provision
provoke
psychological
psychologist
psychology
public
publication
publicly
publish
publishing
pull
punishment
purchase
pure
purely
purpose
pursue
pursuit
push
put
qualification
qualify
qualitative
quality
quantitative
quantity
quarter

question
quick
quickly
quiet
quite
quote
race
racial
racism
radical
radically
radio
rain
raise
random
range
rank
rapid
rapidly
rare
rarely
rate
rather
rating
ratio
rational
raw
reach
react
reaction
read
reader
readily
reading
ready
real
realistic
reality
realize
really
realm
reason
reasonable
reasonably
reasoning
recall
receive
recent
recently
reception
recipient
recognition
recognize
recommend
recommendation
record
recording
recover
recovery
recruit
red
reduce
reduction
refer
reference

reflect
reflection
reform
refuse
regard
regardless
regime
region
regional
register
regular
regularly
regulate
regulation
reinforce
reject
relate
related
relation
relationship
relative
relatively
relax
release
relevance
relevant
reliable
relief
religion
religious
rely
remain
remainder
remark
remarkable
remember
remind
remote
removal
remove
render
rent
repair
repeat
repeated
repeatedly
replace
replacement
reply
report
represent
representation
representative
reproduce
reputation
request
require
requirement
research
researcher
resemble
reserve
reside
residence
resident

resist
resistance
resolution
resolve
resort
resource
respect
respective
respectively
respond
response
responsibility
responsible
rest
restore
restrict
restriction
result
retain
return
reveal
revenue
reverse
review
revise
revision
revolution
revolutionary
reward
rhetoric
rich
ride
right
ring
rise
risk
ritual
rival
river
road
rock
role
roll
romantic
room
root
rough
roughly
round
route
routine
row
rule
run
rural
rush
sacrifice
sad
safe
safety
sake
sale
salt
same
sample

sanction
satellite
satisfaction
satisfactory
satisfy
save
say
scale
scenario
scene
schedule
scheme
scholar
scholarship
school
science
scientific
scientist
scope
score
screen
script
sea
search
season
seat
second
secondary
secondly
secret
section
sector
secure
security
see
seed
seek
seem
seemingly
segment
select
selected
selection
selective
self
sell
semester
seminar
send
senior
sense
sensitive
sensitivity
sentence
separate
separately
separation
sequence
series
serious
seriously
serve
service
session
set

setting
settle
settlement
seven
several
severe
sex
sexual
sexuality
shake
shall
shape
share
sharp
she
sheet
shift
ship
shock
shoot
shop
short
shortly
shot
should
show
shut
sick
side
sight
sign
signal
significance
significant
significantly
signify
silence
similar
similarity
similarly
simple
simplify
simply
simultaneously
since
sing
single
sister
sit
site
situate
situation
six
size
sketch
skill
skilled
skin
sleep
slide
slight
slightly
slip
slow
slowly

small
smile
smoke
smooth
so
social
socially
society
sociology
soft
software
soil
soldier
sole
solely
solid
solution
solve
some
somebody
somehow
someone
something
sometimes
somewhat
somewhere
son
song
soon
sophisticated
sorry
sort
soul
sound
source
south
southern
space
span
spatial
speak
speaker
special
specialist
specie
species
specific
specifically
specify
spectrum
speech
speed
spell
spend
spending
sphere
spin
spirit
spiritual
spite
split
sponsor
sport
spot
spread

spring
square
stability
stable
staff
stage
stake
stance
stand
standard
standing
star
start
state
statement
static
station
statistic
statistical
status
stay
steady
steal
stem
step
stereotype
stick
still
stimulate
stimulus
stock
stone
stop
storage
store
storm
story
straight
straightforward
strain
strand
strange
strategic
strategy
stream
street
strength
strengthen
stress
stretch
strict
strictly
strike
striking
string
strip
strive
strong
strongly
structural
structure
struggle
student
study
stuff

style
subject
subjective
submit
subordinate
subsequent
subsequently
substance
substantial
substantially
substitute
subtle
succeed
success
successful
successfully
successive
such
sudden
suddenly
suffer
sufficient
sufficiently
suggest
suggestion
suit
suitable
sum
summarize
summary
summer
sun
superior
supplement
supply
support
supporter
supportive
suppose
suppress
sure
surely
surface
surprise
surprising
surprisingly
surround
survey
survival
survive
suspect
suspend
sweet
switch
symbol
symbolic
symptom
synthesis
system
systematic
table
tackle
take
tale
talent

talk
tape
target
task
taste
tax
teach
teacher
teaching
team
tear
technical
technique
technological
technology
telephone
television
tell
temperature
temporary
ten
tend
tendency
tension
term
terminology
territory
test
testing
text
textbook
than
thank
that
the
theater
their
them
theme
themselves
then
theoretical
theorist
theory
therapy
there
thereby
therefore
these
thesis
they
thick
thin
thing
think
thinking
third
thirty

this
thoroughly
those
though
thought
thousand
threat
threaten
three
threshold
through
throughout
throw
thus
ticket
tie
tight
time
timing
tiny
tip
title
to
today
together
tomorrow
tone
tonight
too
tool
top
topic
total
totally
touch
tough
tour
toward
towards
town
trace
track
trade
tradition
traditional
traditionally
traffic
train
training
trait
transfer
transform
transformation
transition
translate
translation
transmission
transmit

transport
trap
travel
treat
treatment
tree
trend
trial
trigger
trip
trouble
truly
trust
truth
try
tune
turn
tutor
twelve
twentieth
twenty
twice
two
type
typical
typically
ultimate
ultimately
unable
uncertain
uncertainty
under
undergo
undergraduate
underlie
undermine
understand
understanding
undertake
undoubtedly
unexpected
unfortunately
uniform
union
unique
unit
unite
unity
universal
universe
university
unknown
unless
unlike
unlikely
unnecessary
until
unusual

up
update
upon
upper
upset
urban
urge
us
usage
use
useful
user
usual
usually
utility
valid
validity
valuable
value
van
variable
variation
varied
variety
various
vary
vast
vehicle
venture
verbal
version
versus
vertical
very
via
vice
victim
victory
video
view
viewer
viewpoint
village
violate
violence
violent
virtual
virtually
virtue
visible
vision
visit
visitor
visual
vital
vocabulary
voice
volume

voluntary
volunteer
vote
vulnerable
wage
wait
wake
walk
wall
want
war
warm
warn
warning
wash
waste
watch
water
wave
way
we
weak
weakness
wealth
weapon
wear
weather
web
website
week
weekend
weekly
weigh
weight
welcome
welfare
well
west
western
what
whatever
when
whenever
where
whereas
whereby
wherever
whether
which
while
whilst
white
who
whole
whom
whose
why
wide

widely
widespread
wife
wild
will
willing
win
wind
window
winner
winter
wire
wisdom
wish
with
withdraw
within
without
witness
woman
wonder
wonderful
wood
word
work
worker
working
workplace
workshop
world
worldwide
worry
worth
worthy
would
write
writer
writing
written
wrong
year
yes
yet
yield
you
young
your
yourself
youth
zero
zone

Credits

Text Credits

Pages 17–18, "Life is Fare" Reprinted with permission from Marcia Davis © 2010. **Page 19,** "Animals of the New Mexico Desert" by Betsy Rodman. Reprinted with permission. **Page 23,** "Peter's Beach" by Cabeb Gattegno From Short Passages, by Caleb Gattegno, www.EducationalSolutions.com. **Page 84,** "My Journey with Books" by Shanna Germain. Reprinted with permission. **Page 85,** "View from My Window" by Anoushka Havinden. Reprinted with permission. **Pages 136–137,** "Study Examines the Psychology Behind Students Who Don't Cheat" by Jeff Grabmeier. Research News. The Ohio State University. Reprinted with permission.

References

Reynolds, Scott J. and Tara L. Ceranic. "The Effects of Moral Judgment and Moral Identity on Moral Behavior: An Empirical Examination of the Moral Individual." *Journal of Applied Psychology* 92.6 (Nov. 2007): 1610–1624. Print.

Skatssoon, Judy. "Which Sort of Cheat Are You?" *ABC Science Online Journal* (2005): n. pag. Web. 20 March 2010.

von Hippel, William, Jessica L. Lakin, and Richard J. Shakarchi. "Individual Differences in Motivated Social Cognition: The Case of Self-Serving Information Processing." *Personality and Social Psychology Bulletin* 31 (2005): 1347–1357. Print.

Photo Credits

All photos are used under license from Shutterstock.com except for the following: **Page 19** (bottom) Rick & Nora Bowers/Alamy; **p. 28** (right) Corbis Bridge/Alamy; **p. 48** (left) Richard Green/Commercial/Alamy; **p. 66** Ilene MacDonald/Alamy; **p. 69** (left) Justin Kase z02z/Alamy; **p. 116** Angela Hampton Picture Library/Alamy; **p. 136** Sean Locke/iStockphoto.com; **p. 155** (left) Joseph Project-Malawi/Alamy, (middle) RubberBall/Alamy; **p. 213** (top) Ben Blankenburg/iStockphoto.com.